Math and Logic Puzzles

for PC Enthusiasts

J. J. Clessa

DOVER PUBLICATIONS, INC.
Mineola, New York

Dedicated
(in chronological sequence)
to
S., J.A. and J.E.
from
L.S.C.

Copyright

Published in Canada by General Publishing Company, Ltd., 30 Lesmill Road, Don Mills, Toronto, Ontario.
Published in the United Kingdom by Constable and Company, Ltd., 3 The Lanchesters, 162–164 Fulham Palace Road, London W6 9ER.

Bibliographical Note

This Dover edition, first published by Dover Publications, Inc., in 1996, is a slightly altered republication of the work first published by Pan Books, London, England, 1983, under the title *Micropuzzles* (in the "Pan/Personal Computer News Computer Library"). (Many had been published earlier in the magazine *Personal Computer World*.) In the Dover edition all references to a prize contest associated with the original publication have been removed, including two of the three puzzles offered for that contest. Four new puzzles have been added by the author, raising the total number of puzzles from 63 to 65. A solution has been provided for the one puzzle ("The Hymn Board") retained from the original contest, as well as for all the new puzzles. A few minor errors have been corrected, the author's introduction has been slightly revised and a Publisher's Note written.

Library of Congress Cataloging-in-Publication Data

Clessa, J. J.
    [Micropuzzles]
    Math and logic puzzles for PC enthusiasts / J.J. Clessa.
        p.   cm.
    Originally published: Micropuzzles. London : Pan Books, 1983, in series: Pan/Personal computer news computer library.
    ISBN 0-486-29192-8 (pbk.)
    1. Mathematical recreations—Data processing.   I. Title.
QA95.C55   1996
793.7'4—dc20   96-5615
                                                                    CIP

Manufactured in the United States of America
Dover Publications, Inc., 31 East 2nd Street, Mineola, N.Y. 11501

Publisher's Note

The original edition of this book was published in 1983. That is a long time ago in the world of computer technology, and personal computers were very different then. Moreover, a far larger proportion of those who owned microcomputers (i.e., PCs) were hobbyists who knew how to program their machines than is the case nowadays.

Neither of these facts should prove an obstacle to the enjoyment of the puzzles in this collection.

First of all, a good many of these puzzles require no more than unaided brainpower or at most a pocket calculator. As for those that do require the help of a computer: computers have changed greatly in more than a decade, but in changing they have become much more powerful and so even better suited for problem solving.

For conquering the problems that require computer assistance, you do have to know some simple programming. BASIC, the language used in the examples given in some of the solutions, has survived—in fact, proliferated. Many varieties of BASIC are available in numerous implementations for all major computer platforms. Although an understanding of BASIC helps, we hardly need add that you may use almost any computer language in your own attempts to solve these problems.

Because logic and simple mathematics—and above all thinking—are the major prerequisites for getting the most out of this book, its value has not diminished. Therefore, we have decided to reprint it virtually intact.

By the way, the name 'J. J. Clessa' is a *nom de plume*—an anagram composed of the initials of the author's wife, two daughters, and himself, as this book's dedication will reveal.

Enjoy!

Contents

Introduction

The problems in this book are intended not for the mathematician but for the home computer amateur.

No specialist mathematical knowledge is necessary for the majority of the puzzles – merely a logical mind, the ability to use the microcomputer, and a degree of perseverance. For even the most difficult of the problems, 'O'-level standard in mathematics (equivalent to 12th grade in the United States) should be adequate.

The puzzles are of two types – quickies and more difficult puzzles.

The quickies (which are often more difficult than the so-called 'difficult' problems) should be answered in not more than one minute each, and I warn you that there are several 'trick' answers.

The more difficult puzzles could take quite a bit longer, and I would hope that each one would offer you a pleasant evening's entertainment, and also give you quite a bit of practice in using your microcomputer.

I have enclosed a couple of subroutines to give you the idea:
—one to generate successive primes
– the second to test for a palindromic number

I would suggest that you convert these to your own BASIC language (they were originally written in MBASIC and have been slightly modified for the Dover edition) and make them the start of a library of problem solving routines—to which you could add your own creations as you generate them during the course of solving the problems in this book.

Finally, answers are given to all problems, and where applicable I have given explanation of the method of solution. But—a special plea—if you decide that you can't do any problem, give it one more try before you go to the answer. In that way I guarantee you will maximize the fun you will get from this book.

J. J. Clessa
1983, 1996

Quickies

1

A two-digit number, read from left to right, is 4.5 times as large as the same number read from right to left.

What is the number?

2

Three men are in a restaurant. The bill comes to £30, so each man gives a £10 note to the waiter.

The waiter takes the bill and delivers the payment to the manager – who decides that he's overcharged so he gives the waiter £5 to take back to the men.

On the way back to the table, the waiter dishonestly pockets £2 of the £5 for himself, and give each man £1 back only.

That means that each man has paid £9 – making a total of £27. The waiter has £2, the men have paid £27 . . . that comes to £29.

What has happened to the missing £1?

3

Only one of these five statements is correct – which is it?

(1) Only one of these statements is false.
(2) Only two of these statements are false.
(3) Three of these statements are false.
(4) Four of these statements are false.
(5) All five of these statements are false.

4

Which number when added to 5/4 gives the same result as when it is multiplied by 5/4?

5

Two English coins add up to 55p. One is *not* a 50p piece. What are they? (U.S. and Canadian readers may substitute '¢' for 'p'.)

6

Not so much a problem, more of an outrage. You have only thirty seconds to complete the following Irish crossword, so don't pull any punches.

1	2	3	4	5
2				
3				
4				
5				

Clues across
(1) Hit hard.
(2) A party drink.
(3) Often in seaside shows.
(4) Use for making holes.
(5) What conductors do to tickets.

Clues down
(1) Vegetables.
(2) Female sheep.
(3) They lay eggs.
(4) Often sailed on.
(5) Dropped by Cockneys.

7

A girl has as many sisters as she has brothers. But each brother has twice as many sisters as brothers. How many brothers and sisters in the family?

8

A train leaves Edinburgh at 8.00 a.m. and travels to London at 60 mph. At 9.00 a.m. another train leaves London and travels towards Edinburgh at 90 mph. Which train is the nearer to London when they pass?

9

If the only sister of your mother's only brother has an only child, what would be your relationship to that child?

10

Not a puzzle for the health addict.

A man buys a carton of 200 cigarettes, and every day he smokes seven cigarettes less than the day before. Eventually the day arrives when his quota is down to one cigarette – which happens to be all that there is left in the original carton.

How many a day was he smoking when he bought the carton?

11

An old chestnut.

If a brick weighs seven pounds plus half a brick, what is the weight of a brick and a half?

12

There are eight oranges in a box. How can you divide them between eight people so that each person gets one orange, and one orange is still left in the box?

The oranges must not be peeled or cut.

13

Jack's famous beanstalk doubled its height every day. After twenty-one days it was as high as the town hall. After how many days was it half the height of the town hall?

14

Some ducks are marching across a path. There's a duck in front of two ducks, there's a duck behind two ducks, and there's a duck in the middle of two ducks.

What's the least number of ducks that there could have been?

15

If a hen and a half lay an egg and a half in a day and a half, how long will it take twelve hens to lay twelve eggs?

16

Here's a simple multiplication problem in which each letter represents a different digit. Can you solve it?

IF×
AT
———
FIAT
———

17

How many triangles are there in this figure?

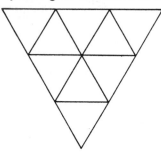

18

One ninth is two less than a third of one half of X. What is X?

19

Which number, when added to twelve, gives the same result as if it were multiplied by six?

20

Which are there more of:

(a) square yards in a square kilometre, or
(b) millimetres in a mile?

21

Write down the next number in this series:

18, 46, 94, 63, 52, ?

22

Rearrange the following letters so as to form one word:

NEW DOOR

23

Two trains approach each other from opposite directions. One is travelling at 50 mph, the other at 70 mph. How far apart are they fifteen minutes before they meet?

24

There's a three digit number which:

if you add seven to it it divides exactly by seven;
if you add eight to it it divides exactly by eight;
if you add nine to it it divides exactly by nine.

What is the number?

25

Write down eleven thousand, eleven hundred, and eleven. It doesn't divide exactly by seven – agreed?

26

There is one word on this page which is spelt incorrectly. Can you find it?

27

A man is standing on a railway line and hears a train coming. He runs for safety as quickly as possible. However, he first runs twenty yards along the track towards the oncoming train. Why?

28

Three boys have twenty conkers (horse chestnuts) between them. Billy has three more conkers than Alan, but five fewer than Charlie. How many conkers do they each have?

29

A snail climbs up a greasy flagpole twenty feet high. He climbs three feet each day but slips back two feet each night. He starts at daybreak on 1st February. When does he reach the top?

30

The big hand of the Big Ben clock weighs 1200 lb, and the hour hand weighs 700 lb. What is the total weight of the hands? The answer is *not* 1900 lb.

31

A man drives to work at 30 mph. How fast would he have to drive back in order to average 60 mph for the two-way journey? The answer is *not* 90 mph.

32

Two women sell 60 lb of tomatoes in the market. The first woman sells half of them at 3 lb for 50p, making £5 in all. The second woman sells the other half at 2 lb for 50p, making £7.50, giving a total of £12.50 between them.

The following week they decide to sell their produce jointly, and so they fix the price at 5 lb for £1. Once again, they have 60 lb to sell. However, when all the tomatoes have been sold they find they have only £12 between them and a quarrel ensues as to where the extra 50p went.

Where did it go?

33

How is it possible to be on board an ocean liner, sailing from Newfoundland to Ireland, and yet to be never more than two miles from the nearest land?

34

Using standard mathematical symbols, e.g. $+$, $-$, $\times$, etc., rearrange four fives to equal the numbers one to ten. For example, $5/5+5-5=1$, $5/5+5/5=2$, etc.

35

A newlaid egg drops six feet directly above a concrete floor without breaking. How is this done? (And it's not hard-boiled.)

36

If it takes four men eight days to dig four holes, how long does it take one man to dig half a hole?

37

Name two Olympic events in which the winner crosses the finishing line facing backwards.

38

What is special about the number 8,549,176,320?

39

There are two stalls in a market selling apples. Stall A sells them at three for 10p, stall B sells them at two for 10p. On Monday, each stall sells 300 apples, therefore stall A collects £10 and stall B collects £15 – a total of £25.

On Tuesday, each stall again has 300 apples, but this time both stalls decide to combine and sell at five for 20p. At the end of the day, all the apples are sold but they find that they only have £24 to be shared between them. What happened to the extra £1?

40

If you could fold a sheet of rice paper one thousandth of an inch thick exactly fifty times, how thick would the resulting wad be?

41

Which weighs the most, a pound of feathers or a pound of gold? The answer is *not* that they both weigh the same.

42

A saucer is floating in a bathtub. Which raises the water level more – dropping a penny into the saucer or into the bathtub?

43

Find the next number in the series:

1, 2, 3, 5, 7, 11, 13, 17, 19, ?

44

A simple number crossword.

Across
(A) A square.
(C) A/3.

Down
(A) B down − C across +22.
(B) Multiple of 13.

45

Find the next letter in the series. (A clue: if you can't do it, ask a five-year-old child.)

A, E, F, H, I, K, L, M, N, ?

46

A man leave his house and walks one mile due north. He then walks one mile due east, followed by one mile due south, when he arrives back at his starting point. How is this possible?

47

Why have no famous women ever been born in London?

48

Another simple number crossword.

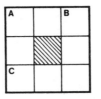

Across
(A) A down −15 (and a multiple of 17).
(C) A beastly number.

Down
(A) A square.
(B) A square +2.

49

Find the next letter in the series:

O, T, T, F, F, S, S, E, ?

50

Find the next number in the series:

1/2, 1, 2, 5, 10, 20, 50, 100, ?

51

A bit harder than usual for a quickie. Find the missing numbers in the series:

10, 11, 12, 13, 14, 15, 16, 17, 20, 22, 24, ?, 100, 121, ?

52

Quickly now, what is

$1 \times 2 \times 3 \times 4 \times 5 \times 6 \times 7 \times 8 \times 9 \times 0$?

53

1	2	3
4	5	6
7	8	9

Can you arrange the digits 1–9 in a 3×3 grid so that all rows, columns, and diagonals add up to the same total?

54

Can you find a word of nine letters from which you can delete one letter at a time and yet always give another valid word, until you get down to a single-letter word? There's no need to rearrange the letters at each stage, either.

55

How many two-digit positive whole numbers are there?

56

At which end – east or west – of the Panama Canal is the Atlantic Ocean?

57

Which is the longest two-word sentence?

58

A very old chestnut.

A bottle and a cork cost 25p. The bottle costs 20p more than the cork. How much does the cork cost?

59

Find four consecutive prime numbers that add up to 220.

60

If ninety-one teams enter the FA Cup, how many matches will be played, not counting replays?

61

Join the nine dots shown using four straight lines only, without taking your pencil off the paper, without passing through any dot more than once, and without retracing any line.

.   ,   ■

.   ■   ■

.   ■   ■

62

A certain family has three children, and half the children are boys. How is this?

63

A woman gave birth to two boys on the same date, within about twenty minutes of each other, and yet they were not twins. How could this be?

64

A rope ladder hangs down the side of a ship. The rungs on the ladder are one foot apart. At low tide the water just covers the bottom rung of the ladder. At high tide, the water level has risen by three feet. How many rungs will be covered by then?

65

Two Indians are walking through the forest. One Indian is the son of the other, but the other is not his father. (Dare I say it:) How?

66

A tramp can make one cigarette from every three cigarette butts that he has. One day, when he is completely without any smokes at all, he finds a packet of ten cigarettes.

How many full cigarettes can he smoke from these?

67

A friend of mine's grandfather is younger than his father. How is this possible?

68

How far can a rabbit run into a wood?

69

A farmer dies and leaves his seventeen cows to his three sons with the following provision:

The eldest son is to receive ½
The second son is to receive ⅓
The youngest son is to receive ⅑

How is the will settled?

70

A driver is driving towards a level crossing at 60 mph. At the same time a train is hurtling towards the same crossing at 60 mph. They are both 100 metres from the crossing when the driver realises that his brakes have failed. How does he get across?

Micropuzzles

1 Pythagoras for beginners

There's a well-known story about an old Sioux Indian tribe that lived on a reservation in the north of Canada. It was a status symbol in this tribe to own a rug made from the skin of some rare animal, and the rarer the animal, the more impressive was the status of the owner. Well, various members of the tribe owned deerskin rugs, several had buffalo, some had bison, but only one had a hippopotamus rug, and that was the witch-doctor's wife. She was a rather heavy woman with an unpleasant arrogant manner who frequently infuriated other members of the tribe with her superior airs and graces.

One hot summer's day, all the ladies were outside their teepees sitting on their fancy rugs, when the witch-doctor's wife began her usual boasting about how superior she was to the others, and how her husband was the most influential member of the tribe, even more influential than the chief himself. It was too much for two of the other squaws, they called for their teenage sons and told them to go across to the witch-doctor's wife and throw her into the river. Unfortunately, this was more easily said than done, and the fracas finished up with the two young braves being thrown into the river.

What's the point of this long boring tale? you may ask. Well, it just proves that the squaw on the hippopotamus was equal to the sons of the squaws on the other two hides!

Now for the micropuzzle. A Pythagorean triangle is a right-angled triangle whose sides are an exact number of units in length, and of course conform to the famous rule that the square on the hypotenuse is equal to the sum of the squares on the other two sides. Probably the best-known Pythagorean triangle has sides of 3, 4, and 5 units respectively, and, of course, 3 squared plus 4 squared equals 5 squared. The area of such a triangle is obtained by multiplying the lengths of the two smaller sides and dividing the answer by two. The perimeter of the triangle is the total distance round it, i.e. the sum of all three sides. So, in our 3-4-5 triangle, the area is 6 square units, and the perimeter is 12 units.

I'd like you to find the smallest-area Pythagorean triangle whose perimeter is a perfect square and whose area is a perfect cube.

2 Flying the Glasgow shuttle

By the way, in the last puzzle I mentioned two animals, the buffalo and the bison, which I suppose everyone's heard of, but I wonder how many of you know the difference between a buffalo and a bison?

It's very simple really – you can't wash your face in a buffalo. I suppose that's quite logical when you think about it, and of course, it brings me on to the next puzzle, which also requires a bit of logic for its solution.

On the London–Glasgow air shuttle are three passengers named Brown, Jones, and Smith. By coincidence, the pilot, co-pilot, and cabin steward on the aircraft are also named Brown, Jones, and Smith, but not necessarily respectively.

(1) Passenger Jones earns £5,200 per annum.
(2) The cabin steward lives midway between London and Glasgow.
(3) Smith, the crew member, is married to the co-pilot's sister.
(4) The passenger with the same last name as the cabin steward lives in Glasgow.
(5) The passenger who lives nearest to the cabin steward earns exactly three times as much per week as the cabin steward.
(6) Passenger Brown lives in London.

What is the pilot's surname?

3 A chessboard dilemma

I don't know if you are aware of the paradox of the Christian working for a Jewish company (funny, it's never the other way round, is it?). One day he went to ask his employer for a raise and received the following reply.

'Let me see, Fred,' said the boss. 'You work here eight hours a day, that's a third of the day, and since this year is a leap year, that means that you will work one third of the year, i.e. 366/3=122 days. Now, you don't work on Sundays, since that's your Sabbath, and you don't work on Saturday's, since that's mine, which amounts to 104 days for the weekends, so that leaves eighteen days. Now, you take a day off each for Christmas, New Year, Easter, and the Spring Bank Holiday, which leaves fourteen days, and since you get a fortnight's annual holiday once a year, it seems to me that you don't work here at all.'

I suppose that's no worse than some of the 'quickies' that you'll find elsewhere in this book, but I don't intend to explain it. If you can't sort it out, then ask your dad, it must be at least as old as he is, whoever you are.

Here's a puzzle that's got a little more substance to it than that.

Place eight coins or tokens on the squares of a standard
chessboard so that no two are in line horizontally, vertically, or
diagonally. In addition, no coin may occupy a square on either
main diagonal of the board. In other words, only the unshaded
squares in the diagram may be used. If you really feel smart,
there are two solutions and you can try to find both of them.

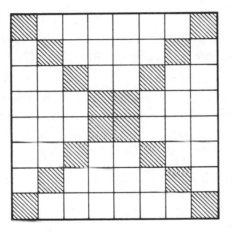

4 A palindromic puzzle

I suppose everyone knows what a palindrome is, but in case anyone doesn't, I'm going to tell you. It's a word (or even a whole sentence) that reads the same backwards as it does forwards – for example, OXO, or PEEP.

Now, this puzzle is about palindromic numbers not palindromic words, i.e. numbers which read the same from right to left, and from left to right.

Three friends, Alan, Bert, and Colin, each possess vehicles. Alan owns a big foreign car, Bert a small English car, and Colin has a moped.

One day, while discussing mileages, Alan reports that his mileometer, which gives six-figure mileage readings, is currently showing a palindromic reading of 006600 miles. 'What a coincidence!' exclaims Bert. 'So is mine. The five-figure reading at the moment is 18981 miles.'

'Well I never,' says Colin. 'Although the mileometer on my moped only allows four figures, it's reading 5335 miles, which is also palindromic. I wonder if we're ever likely to get such a coincidence again.'

Well, of course, since each vehicle does a different weekly mileage from the others, there's no way in which the question could be answered. But supposing all three mileometers were connected to just one vehicle, and also supposing that they were equally accurate, then what is the least number of miles that would need to elapse before:

(a) Alan's and Bert's mileometers were both showing palindromic readings again?
(b) Alan's and Colin's mileometers were both showing palindromic readings again?
(c) Bert's and Colin's mileometers were both showing palindromic readings again?
(d) All three mileometers were mutually palindromic again?

5 Digital dexterity

This puzzle is a little bit harder than most, and you should stand by for some rather large numbers which, I suppose, will virtually exclude most micro solutions. Just as well, since they'd probably take weeks, or years to compute the solution.

However, like almost all the problems in this book, it is not beyond the scope of 'O'-level mathematics (12th-grade in the U.S.). There are several parts to this problem.

A certain number ends in the digit 'a'. When the 'a' is taken from the end of the number and placed at the beginning, a new number is formed which is 'a' times the original number.

What are the original numbers if:

(1) 'a' = 2?
(2) 'a' = 3?
(3) 'a' = 4?
(4) 'a' = 5?
(5) 'a' = 6?
(6) 'a' = 7?
(7) 'a' = 8?
(8) 'a' = 9?

To avoid any ambiguity, I'll give an example. Suppose we look at the first problem where 'a'=2. If the number you are considering is 1312, then by transferring the '2' from the end of the number to the front, the new number 2131 is formed. Unfortunately, 2131 does not equal two times 1312 and hence 1312 is not the correct solution, but we're sure you'll find an answer that is. Please give the smallest answer in each case if more than one is possible.

6 A palindromic square

As you should be well aware (if you've bothered to read the preamble in an earlier problem), a palindrome is a word which reads the same backwards as it does forwards. For example, 'noon', 'anna', 'deed' are all palindromic words.

If you want to get very clever, then you can create entire sentences which are palindromic, such as the phrase that Adam was reputed to have said to Eve on their first encounter:

Madam I'm Adam.

I am informed by reliable sources that her predictable reply was: 'Eve.' There's also the famous phrase that Napoleon said when his wife visited him in exile:

Able was I ere I saw Elba.

On to the current puzzle, which is once again about palindromic numbers. The numbers 121 and 484 have the property that they are palindromic (i.e. read the same from right to left as from left to right), and they both happen to be perfect squares. They each contain an odd number of digits (three).

I'd like you to find the smallest palindromic number that is also a perfect square, but which contains an even number of digits.

7 More perfect squares

Before I give you this puzzle, here is a rather surprising fact on which you might be able to make a few bob in the way of a wager.

Did you know that, if there are twenty-three people in a room, it is better than even money that at least two of them will have the same birthday. For example, suppose you are in the bar of your local, and there are at least twenty-two other people in the bar with you, you would be on a pretty good bet to wager that at least two people present have the same birthday (i.e. day and month, not date of birth).

If there are more than thirty people the odds increase to about 75%, and if there are sixty, then it's a racing certainty, if you can find someone daft enough (or drunk enough) to take the bet.

This fact is particularly applicable to classes in school, where not only will there be two kids with the same birthday, but they'll also (likely as not) have the same date of birth.

All that has nothing whatever to do with the next puzzle, but it's a useful (or useless) piece of information which will make you the genius of the pub or the cocktail party for one night at least. Now, at last, for the puzzle.

Find the smallest perfect square that is also the average of two other perfect squares. In other words, find three perfect squares A, B, and C such that

$$B = (A+C)/2.$$

Oh yes, one other stipulation to curtail all the smart-alecs: A, B, and C may not be equal.

8 A question of logic

A natural and really quite obvious variation on a dodge shown elsewhere in this book for squaring numbers that end in 5 is the trick of squaring numbers that end in ½.

Take the number to be squared, and ignore the ending ½.

Multiply the whole-number portion by the whole-number portion plus one, and add ¼ to the result.

Let's use an example. Consider the square of 3½. Ignore the ½ and multiply 3 by 3+1 giving 12. Add ¼ to the product and the answer is 12¼.

And now to something more difficult. You won't solve this one with a simple 'dodge', but a bit of logical thought should get you to the answer.

A child's cube has coloured faces. Five colours only are used: red, green, blue, yellow, and orange.

Three views of the same cube are shown here, and in each of the views, the colour on the bottom face of the cube is not repeated on any other face.

Which colour occurs twice on the cube?

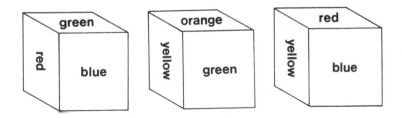

9 The whole truth and nothing but the truth

This next puzzle is another question of logic. There is a famous island in the Pacific Ocean (whose name I forget) on which there live three tribes:

– the Whites, who always tell the truth;
– the Blacks, who always tell lies;
– and the Greys, who lie and tell the truth alternately (although their first answer may be either truth or lie).

These natives always gather in groups of three, with one representative of each tribe in the group.

A visitor to the island approached such a group of three natives, and had the following conversation with the first native.

'Are you the White, the Black, or the Grey?'

'I am the Grey.'

'And what about your friend here?'

'He is a Black.'

'So your other friend is the White?'

'Of course.'

Was the 'other friend' a White, and if not, what was he?

10 Talking turkey

You heard the one about the market where the chickens were going cheap? (Never mind if you haven't, it's not a great loss.) Now here's a pretty 'fowl' problem.

A turkey farmer has 100 cages ranged in the form of a continuous circle around the perimeter of his farm. The cages are numbered clockwise sequentially from 1 to 100, with cage number 100 completing the circle and immediately adjacent to cage number 1. In each cage is a turkey.

The farmer decides to kill one turkey only per month, and in order to make his monthly selection, he counts clockwise N birds from the cage of last month's victim (N being the number of days in that month) to obtain his current month's turkey dinner.

Assuming his first bird comes from cage number 31 in January 1980, then

(a) Which will be the last bird to be eaten?
(b) Which bird will be Christmas dinner in 1985?

Note that the count is made on *birds*, not cages.

11 The not-so-perfect square

A simple but useful device this time. How to square a number that ends in 5. I can remember my army days (that dates me, doesn't it?), when I used to win bets in the NAAFI (ask your dad if you don't know what that is) that I could square a number that ended with 5 quicker in my head than it could be done with pencil and paper. When you know this trick, you'll be able to do it too.

Take the number, and forget the final 5. Suppose the remaining digits make up the number X. Then multiply X by X+1 and put 25 on to the end of the product. This gives the required answer.

It's easier to demonstrate. Suppose we wish to square the number 205. Ignore the final 5, this gives 20. Multiply 20 by 20+1, i.e. $20 \times 21 = 420$. And put 25 at the end of the product. This gives 42025, which is 205×205.

Another example, 95 squared. Drop the 5, leaving 9. Multiply 9 by 10 giving 90, and put 25 after it. This gives the required answer, 9025.

Now for the next puzzle. It's not quite as easy as it looks. In fact when it first appeared in *Personal Computer World*, many readers thought it wasn't soluble. So try to think laterally.

A certain perfect square has the property that, if 5 is added to it, a second perfect square is obtained, and if 5 is subtracted from it, a third perfect square is obtained.

What is the original perfect square?

12 Squaring the cube

We showed you a simple trick which you can do with your friends in the previous problem. Here's another one which is probably not quite so well known.

Ask anyone to write down their telephone number. Tell them to scramble the digits any way they like to create another number. They should then subtract the smaller of the two numbers from the larger.

Ask them then to cross out one digit from this answer, and then to add up the remaining ones and tell you the total. You can then tell them the digit they crossed out by subtracting the value they gave you from the next highest multiple of 9.

For example, let us suppose the telephone number is 686174, which is then scrambled to give another number, 461768. The difference between the two is 224406. Cross out one digit from this value, say the 4, and add up the rest to give 14. By subtracting 14 from 18 (the next highest multiple of 9) you get the digit crossed out, i.e. 4.

If a 0 or 9 is crossed out, you can't be sure which it was, but you could prevent this by asking them to cross out any digit except zero.

Short and sweet is this next puzzle, but you may not find it short and sweet to obtain the answer.

Two numbers, A and B, are made up from the digits 0 through 9, using each digit once and once only. The cube of one of the numbers is equal to the square of the other, i.e. A squared = B cubed. What are the numbers?

13 A natural mistake

Here's a story that you might not have heard before (and then again, you might have).

Half a dozen ostriches were standing in a circle with their heads stuck in the sand. Up gallops another ostrich into the middle of the circle, looks around, and says, 'Where is everybody?' Ah well, never mind, I'll try to do better next time.

A not-too-difficult puzzle, this one, providing you let the micro do the slogging, which is what this book is all about.

A woman goes into a supermarket and purchases four items. Before she goes to the check-out, she decides to work out the total cost using her new pocket calculator.

However, she is neither numerate, nor very adept in the use of the calculator, because by mistake she hits the 'multiply' key instead of the 'add' key. The result she arrives at is £7.11, and when she reaches the check-out, the assistant adds up the items in the normal way and gets the result £7.11.

Naturally the woman is satisfied, and pays, never knowing the stupid blunder that she has made. (It just shows how dead lucky women are, and it also makes this story rather superfluous.)

What was the cost of each item that she purchased?

14 Ten-digit perfect squares

This puzzle should require a little more initiative than usual, since most micros will only handle numbers up to seven or eight digits (although you fellows with PASCAL systems, or CPM BASIC, should be able to cope).*

There are ten parts to the problem.

(a) Which ten-digit perfect square contains the most zeros?

(b) Which ten-digit perfect square contains the most ones?

(c) Which ten-digit perfect square contains the most twos?

And so on, up to:

(j) Which ten-digit perfect square contains the most nines?

If more than one answer is possible for any part of the puzzle, then any of the possibilities will do.

*[Editor's note, 1996: It is probably unnecessary to mention that, with today's hardware and software, few machines would have difficulty handling this problem.]

15 A bad connection

The other day, while trying to phone the offices of that
prestigious publication, *Personal Computer World*, I got a
crossed line and found myself listening, inadvertently, to the
following conversation between two people who I'll call A and B.

Unfortunately, the line was very bad, and I missed a few parts of
what was said because of the crackles.

(A) 'I've just spent exactly £2 on a mixture of 12p, 14p, and 17p
  stamps.'
(B) 'How many of each did you buy?'
(A) 'I'll not tell you that, but altogether there were ... (CRACKLE)
  ... stamps.'
(B) 'In that case I'll work it out ... wait a minute, I still can't tell
  how many of each you got. Did you buy only one of one
  kind?'
(A) '... (CRACKLE) ...'
(B) 'In that case you bought ...'

At that point the line went dead. Unfortunately, at the two key
points in the conversation, a crackle on the line prevented me
from hearing the full story, but I'm sure you'll be able to tell me,
without any further information, just how many stamps of each
value were bought.

16 A numerical traverse

And now a puzzle to get the micros ticking.

Starting at the square marked 'Start' (would you believe?) and
moving either east, north-east, or south-east with each move

(assume north is at the top of the grid), make twelve moves and reach the square marked 'Finish'.

Add up the numbers in the eleven squares traversed to give a total, A.

Then repeat the performance without entering any square used by the first move (except 'Start' and 'Finish', of course).

Again, add up the numbers in the squares traversed, to give a second total, B.

The problem is to find the two routes which give the greatest difference in values between A and B.

Use the values in the squares to describe the two routes (e.g. Start-2-14-3-18-, etc.), and state the two totals A and B as well as the overall difference.

						10						
					14	5	3					
				18	15	3	9	5				
			1	13	19	7	2	18	9			
		18	9	15	13	11	5	2	11	1		
	8	2	3	3	7	18	12	16	1	17	8	
start	2	14	3	18	7	5	14	6	4	9	17	finish
	2	9	8	2	19	14	18	2	18	15	1	
		18	18	5	7	9	19	16	10	8		
			1	14	2	2	16	2	5			
				2	13	17	13	13				
					6	2	9					
						13						

17 A problem of check-digits

This puzzle is all about check-digits, so we'd better make sure that we all know what a check-digit is, and how it works.

To find the check-digit of modulo 97 for a six-digit number, proceed as follows:

— multiply the first digit of the number by a specific value which is called a weight – W1;
— multiply the second digit of the number by a second weight – W2;
— multiply the third digit by the weight W3, and so on for all six digits;
— add the six products together to give a single total;
— divide this total by 97, and the remainder is the required check-digit.

For example, suppose our weights are 10, 20, 30, 40, 50, and 60, respectively, and suppose we wish to find a check-digit for the number 987654.

Then we calculate:

$(9 \times 10) + (8 \times 20) + (7 \times 30) + (6 \times 40) + (5 \times 50) + (4 \times 60)$
$= 1190.$

1190 leaves a remainder of 26 when divided by 97. Hence the required check-digit is 26.

Right, now for the problem. We are given nine numbers, and check-digits for eight of them. You have simply to calculate the check-digit for the ninth number.

The numbers are as follows, with the check-digits following in brackets:

(1) 693847 (16)
(2) 264315 (27)
(3) 927064 (32)
(4) 472289 (14)
(5) 838521 (73)
(6) 741318 (69)
(7) 553846 (14)
(8) 385132 (10)
(9) 123456 (??)

I'll give you a little more information.

All weights are positive integers between 0 and 99 inclusive.

From left to right across the six digits, the weights are multiples of successive prime numbers (not counting 1 as a prime). For example, if weight W1 is 5, then weight W2 is a multiple of 7, W3 is a multiple of 11, W4 is a multiple of 13, W5 is a multiple of 17, and W6 is a multiple of 19.

This information should render the problem almost trivial. It should certainly bring it well within the range of those micros.

So, I want to know the check-digit of the ninth number.

18 Ceremonial rice pudding

This problem could set a few micros whirring. Every four years, in the village of Poorihana in Burma, the rice-piling ceremony takes place at the appointed hour on the given feast day. (If you believe that, you'll believe anything – Ed.)

When the ceremony begins, one grain of rice is placed in a chosen spot outside the witch-doctor's hut. Exactly one hour later, two grains are added; after a further hour, three more grains are added, and so on – every hour, one more grain is added to the quantity that was added at the previous hour.

The ceremony continues non-stop until there are exactly enough grains to give each of the 23 poorest villagers a square meal, i.e. a meal consisting of a quantity of rice that is a perfect square – each of the 23 villagers receiving exactly the same as each other.

Assuming that each ceremony ends before the next one begins, what is the number of rice grains that each of the 23 villagers receive?

19 Who's who

Funny things, digits – the number kind, I mean. Here's a simple trick with digits that can be quite impressive to anyone not in the know.

Get someone to write down a three-digit number whose digits are different (say, 842).

Now ask him to reverse the digits to give another three-digit number (e.g. 248).

Subtract the smaller of the two numbers from the larger (giving $842 - 248 = 594$).

Now reverse the digits of the result and add to the result (giving $594 + 495 = 1089$).

The answer will always be 1089.

Short and sweet, this puzzle. It's all a matter of logic.

Messrs Baker, Cooper, Parson, and Smith are a baker, a cooper, a parson, and a smith. However, no one has the same name as his vocation.

The cooper is not the namesake of Mr Smith's vocation; the baker is neither Mr Parson nor is he the namesake of Mr Baker's vocation.

What is Mr Baker's vocation?

20 Word frustration

This puzzle will probably be too difficult for all those readers who don't have alpha facilities on their calculators. On the other hand, knowing the ingenuity and facility for invention that this readership possesses, I can't be 100% sure of that, so here goes.

(1) The forty-nine letters shown in the grid can be formed into seven seven-letter words, and the initial letters of each of the seven words will form an eighth word which is the required answer to the puzzle.

(2) Alongside each letter is also a number in the range 1–6. This number indicates the number of squares that must be traversed to reach the next square.

(3) Starting with the letter D in the centre of the grid, move the number of squares specified (in this case six) east, west, north, or south and you will arrive at another square. (Assume north is at the top of the grid.)

(4) If any move takes you beyond the edge of the grid, you should assume that the grid 'wraps around'. Thus, if a northerly move takes you to the top of the grid, the count of squares should continue from the foot of the same column.

(5) Hence, from the start point, a move of six squares east will take you to the right-hand edge after three squares, and the fourth, fifth, and sixth squares should be made from the left-hand edge of the same row to bring you to the letter R2.

(6) In this way, the initial move can take you to either the R2, E2, N3, or S1 squares immediately adjacent to the start letter.

(7) No square may be landed on more than once. Diagonal moves are not permitted.

(8) A correct series of moves throughout the grid will yield seven consecutive seven-letter English words, the initial letters of which, taken in order, will then give the required single-word solution.

T_4	R_6	E_3	S_6	T_5	S_6	O_5
U_2	Y_3	L_4	S_2	O_5	N_2	A_3
R_5	B_3	S_1	E_2	E_1	R_2	N_5
Y_6	L_5	R_2	D_6	N_3	D_2	I_1
E_5	A_4	T_6	S_1	B_3	N_5	G_5
A_3	E_2	E_5	A_2	T_3	G_4	R_6
Y_2	A_1	T_1	T_3	R_3	N_1	I_6

Can you find the single-word solution?

21 A positional problem

This puzzle lends itself to a micro-based solution, although a nifty bit of logical thought and programming will be required.

(1) Select any eight squares from the sixty-four squares in the diagram so that no two are lying on the same diagonal line.
(2) Add the values in the squares chosen to give a total.
(3) The object is to choose the eight squares which yield the highest total.

1	2	3	2	6	8	7	2
8	6	2	5	1	3	1	4
7	1	5	4	2	5	6	8
2	8	4	7	5	1	4	3
4	3	7	2	3	8	5	1
6	5	6	3	4	7	8	3
3	7	1	8	6	2	4	6
8	4	5	6	7	5	1	7

22 Generating a specific value

(1) Using the digits 1–6 inclusive and using each digit once only, form two numbers x and y.

(2) Calculate:
   Sum, S=x+y.
   Difference, D=x−y.
   Product, P=x×y.
   Quotient, Q=x/y.

(3) Finally, evaluate the expression:
   E=P×D−Q×S.

(4) The object is to choose x and y to give the largest possible value of E.

(5) Thus, suppose the numbers chosen were x=1234 and y=56, then:

S=1290
D=1178
P=69104
Q=22.03571

and E=81,376,086. (Give E as a rounded integer.)

Answers should give x, y, and E.

23 Sums of squares

(1) Using the integers 1–79 inclusive, generate perfect squares as follows:

(a) Each perfect square must be the sum of two or more of the seventy-nine given integers.
(b) Any perfect square may only be generated once.
(c) Each of the seventy-nine given integers may be used once only.

(2) Score three points for each perfect square that is the sum of two of the integers; score four points for each perfect square that is the sum of three of the integers; score five points for each perfect square that is the sum of four of the integers; and so on.

(3) Deduct from the total score one point for each unused integer.

(4) All you have to do is to score the highest number of points that you can.

24 A very prime word

(1) Find the largest prime number which, when its digits are translated into characters, gives an English word.

(2) Translate as follows:

0=R	5=N
1=D	6=I
2=A	7=S
3=G	8=T
4=B	9=E

(3) The word must be an entry, or the derivative of an entry, in the *Concise Oxford Dictionary*, fifth edition, and no foreign words or proper nouns are permitted.

25 Fieldcraft

Here's a puzzle which can be solved by micro, but you may find
an easier way.

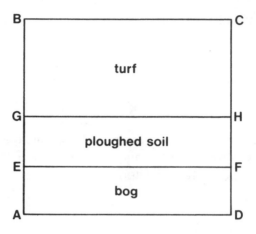

The diagram represents a square field with 600 ft sides.

(1) In the field are three types of surface: turf, ploughed soil, and
bog.
(2) The rectangular section AEFD is bog – AE is 100 ft wide.
(3) The section EGHF is ploughed soil – EG is 200 ft wide.
(4) The remaining section, GBCH, is turf – BG is, of course, 300
ft.
(5) A farmer starts at point A to get to C. He can travel at 2.5
ft/sec in bog, 5 ft/sec on ploughed soil, and 10 ft/sec on turf.

What is the shortest time (to the nearest second) in which the
farmer can get to C?

26 Opening day at the local

Here's a puzzle to test your powers of logic – or maybe even your micro, that is, if you have enough imagination to be able to write a program to solve this problem.

(1) In a village near to my home, there are three pubs only:

The White Swan
The Black Bull
The Grey Goose

(2) On Sundays all the pubs are closed.
(3) The White Swan opens five days a week. The Black Bull opens four days a week. The Grey Goose opens three days a week.
(4) The White Swan is never open four days running. The Black Bull is never open three days running. The Grey Goose is never open two days running.
(5) During a three-day period, the white Swan was closed on the third day, the Black Bull was closed on the second day, and the Grey Goose was closed on the first day.
(6) On Saturdays, and on Mondays, at least one pub is closed.

Assuming that days of opening are regular each week, on which day are all the pubs open?

27 A very charitable dilemma

The members of a philanthropic family decided to donate £2,000 to a group of worthy charities. Each member contributed an equal portion of the money and then allocated it among the agreed charities so that:

(a) Each charity received a donation of at least £1 but no more than £12 from each member.
(b) No two charities received the same amount from the same family member.
(c) No two family members followed the same donation pattern.
(d) All donations were in whole numbers of pounds, and all the money was distributed.

How many family members were there, and how many charities?

28 Cows, pigs and horses

Now for another exercise in logic.

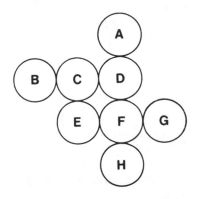

(1) There are eight pens, labelled A to H as shown, and each pen contains either a cow, a horse, a pig, or a sheep.
(2) At least one of each type of animal is present.
(3) At least one pig is penned between two cow pens.
(4) Every horse is penned between two pig pens.
(5) No cow is penned next to a horse.
(6) There is only one sheep, and its pen is not next to that of a pig.
(7) At least two pig pens are contiguous.

Which pen is the sheep in?

29 An exact number of factors

This puzzle can be solved analytically, if you know how, but at the same time it lends itself ideally to solution by micro, if your analytical powers are not so hot.

There are two parts to the problem.

(1) Find the smallest number that has exactly 104 factors, i.e. 104 different numbers that it divides by – including the number itself, but excluding unity.

Thus, for example, the number 12 has exactly five factors: 2, 3, 4, 6, and 12.

(2) Find the smallest odd number that has exactly 104 factors.

30 Cubes and squares

Here's a simple arithmetical dodge that will be of use to those of you who can add but have difficulty with multiplication. It's a method of multiplying by adding (which is all that multiplication really is anyway).

I think it's best illustrated by an example. Suppose we wish to multiply 37 by 23. Then the steps are as follows:

(1)	37	×	23	
(2)	18	×	46	*
(3)	9	×	92	
(4)	4	×	184	*
(5)	2	×	368	*
(6)	1	×	736	

Step (1) 37×23 (which we don't want to do).
Step (2) Halve 37 and ignore the fraction, and double the 23.
Step (3) Halve 18 and double the 46.
Step (4) Halve 9 and ignore the fraction, and double the 92.
Step (5) Halve 4 and double the 184.
Step (6) Halve 2 and double the 368.

Now add up each element on the right side, where the left side is an odd number (i.e. ignore all the entries marked with an asterisk). This gives 23+92+736=851, which is the required answer. Try it with other values. It always works.

Very short to state, this puzzle.

Using the ten digits 0–9, construct two numbers such that the first is the cube, and the second is the fourth power of the same number x. What is x?

31 A question of remainders

Right, now for a problem that is well within the scope of those of you with micros, or even programmable calculators.

If you divided 2519 by 10, there is a remainder of 9.

If you divide 2519 by 9, there is a remainder of 8.

If you divide 2519 by 8, there is a remainder of 7, and so on.

Can you find two other numbers with the same property?

32 A problem of prime factors

Another puzzle for which it is relatively easy to 'bash out' a solution using a micro, or programmable calculator. However, as with quite a few of the others, a little analytical thought can save your hard-ware and tear.

What is the largest number whose prime factors (excluding unity) add up to exactly 100?

Just to be sure that we're all on the same system, the prime factors of 12 are 2, 2, and 3 (since $2\times2\times3=12$). Their sum is 7. Similarly, the prime factors of 90 are 2, 3, 3, and 5, and their sum is 13.

33 The ladies of the committee

A puzzle in logical thought this time, although you can use any means you wish, heuristic methods included (for the uninitiated, that means trial-and-error).

Six ladies are eligible for the offices of Captain, Vice-captain, and Treasurer (in descending order of seniority), in the local ladies' golf club.

(1) Audrey won't serve if Elaine is Captain, or if Freda is Treasurer.
(2) Betty won't be Treasurer if Cynthia is one of the officials.
(3) Audrey won't serve with both Betty and Elaine.
(4) Freda won't serve if Elaine is also an official.
(5) Betty refuses to be Vice-captain.
(6) Freda won't serve if she outranks Audrey.
(7) Cynthia won't serve with Audrey or Betty unless she is Captain.
(8) Doris won't serve unless Betty is Captain.
(9) Betty won't serve with Doris unless Elaine is also an official.
(10) Elaine won't serve unless she or Audrey is Captain.

How can the three offices be filled?

34 An unusual number

A fairly straightforward problem, this time. Readily solvable by the chip-based number-cruncher.

I want you to find a six-digit number which, when multiplied by an integer between 2 and 9 inclusive, gives the original six-digit number with its digits reversed.

Thus, if the original number was 123456, and the chosen integer is 8, then 123456×8 should equal 654321, which, of course, it doesn't. However, it is possible to find more than one solution to this problem, but I'll accept any one that meets the required condition.

35 Tadpoles, terrapins, tortoises, and turtles

A problem involving indeterminate equations, which shouldn't be too difficult to solve with a little bit of programming skill.

Tadpoles cost 59p each. Terrapins cost £1.99 each. Tortoises cost £2.87, and turtles cost £3.44.

£100 exactly has to be spent on the purchase of 100 of these creatures. (Ugh!)

How many of each kind can be bought?

36 More cubes and squares

Before we go on to the latest puzzle, you may be interested in another simple arithmetical trick.

Ask a friend to give you a three-digit number.

Tell him to form a six-digit number by repeating the three digits.

Now ask him to divide the six-digit number by 13 and not to worry about any remainder because there won't be one.

Then ask him to divide the result by 11 and not to worry about any remainder because once again there won't be one.

Then tell him to divide the result by 7 and once again you can assure him that there won't be any remainder.

Finally, you can now tell him that the result he has left will be his original three-digit number.

How can you be sure? Well, it's easy really. When you repeat the three-digit number to form a six-digit number you are really multiplying it by 1001, and 1001 factorizes into $13 \times 11 \times 7$.

Let's give an example. Suppose the number is 123. Then the six-digit number will be 123123 (which is the result you get if you multiply 123 by 1001).

Dividing 123123 by 13 gives 9471 exactly.

Dividing 9471 by 11 gives 861 exactly.

And dividing 861 by 7 gives 123 exactly – which is the number that was originally given.

It's easy when you know how. The following puzzle isn't as simple, but it can be solved with a bit of effort on your home computer.

By subtracting two million from a perfect cube, a number is obtained which is itself the square of one of the factors of two million. All numbers are positive integers.

What is the factor?

37 Sums of cubes

It can be easily shown that the sum of any number of consecutive cubes, starting at 1, is always a perfect square.

Thus:

$1^3+2^3=9=3^2$

$1^3+2^3+3^3=36=6^2$

$1^3+2^3+3^3+4^3=100=10^2$

and so on.

However, in this puzzle, starting at 1 is not permitted.

I want you to find the smallest perfect square that is the sum of at least four consecutive perfect cubes (excluding unity).

That should make the micros whirr.

38 Coconuts galore

This puzzle is based on an old chestnut – or should I say coconut?

Six men are shipwrecked on a desert island. The only food on the island is coconuts. They therefore decide at the outset to pick all the coconuts and divide them equally among themselves.

They spend one complete day gathering all the coconuts into a single pile, and by the time sunset arrives they are so tired that they decide to postpone the share-out until the following day, And so, they all go off to sleep.

During the night, one man awakens and decides to take his share and hide it before the others awake. He divides the pile into six equal shares and finds that there is one coconut remaining, which he throws to a nearby monkey. He then hides his share, puts the rest back into a single pile, and goes back to sleep.

A little later, a second man awakes, and repeats exactly the same process, again finding one coconut remaining after the division, which he throws to the monkey. He also takes and hides his share and goes back to sleep.

This performance is repeated by each man in turn during the night. On each occasion, the coconuts are divided into six, and each time there is one left over which is given to the monkey.

Next morning, all six men awake and decide to share out the remaining coconuts. Again, they divide them into six equal shares, and again there is one coconut left over which is given to the monkey.

What is the least number of coconuts that there could have been in the first place?

39 More trouble with remainders

A certain number, greater than 5,000 but less than 50,000, has the following properties:

– when divided by 4 it gives a remainder of 3;
– when divided by 5 it gives a remainder of 1;
– when divided by 7 it gives a remainder of 2;
– when divided by 11 it gives a remainder of 2;
– when divided by 17 it gives a remainder of 12.

What is the number?

40 Ball-bearing pyramids

I made a mistake when I first published this puzzle in *PCW* 'Leisure Lines' of November 1982, so let's hope I can avoid that this time.

36,894 one-inch-diameter ball-bearings are to be stacked in the form of a pyramid, or cross-section of a pyramid.

The pyramid can be one of three types:

(1) A triangular pyramid in which each ball rests on three beneath it, and in which each layer is in the form of a triangle.
(2) A square pyramid in which each ball rests on four balls beneath it, and in which each layer is in the form of a square.
(3) A rectangular pyramid in which each ball also rests on four others, but in which each layer is in the form of a rectangle.

All the ball-bearings must be used. What type of pyramid can be made, and assuming it has more than one layer, how many layers does it have, and what area of ground does it cover?

There, I hope I've got it right this time.

41 Sums of primes, etc.

This puzzle isn't too easy, but there are bound to be some of you who won't agree with me.

Every odd number, except two, between 1 and 8999 is either a prime or the sum of a prime and twice a square.

For example,

$321 = 19 + 2.1^2$

$27 = 19 + 2.2^2$

$55 = 5 + 2.5^2$

What are the two exceptions?

42 The numerate marathon runner

Runners in a marathon race are assigned consecutive numbers starting at 1.

One of the entrants with a mathematical bent noticed that the sum of the numbers less than his own number was equal to the sum of the numbers greater.

If there were more than 100 runners but less than 1000, what number was he and how many runners were there in the race?

43 Ten-digit primes

This puzzle should certainly stretch your micros – partly
because of the length of the numbers involved, and partly
because of the fact that they are primes, and therefore not
capable of automatic generation. (Did someone say they'd
found a formula?)

There are ten parts to the problem;

(a) Which ten-digit prime number contains the most zeros?
(b) Which ten-digit prime number contains the most ones?
(c) Which ten-digit prime contains the most twos?

And so on, up to nines.

By the way, leading zeros are not permitted.

44 Approximations

X and Y are integers. Use them to generate:

A=X+Y (addition)

B=X−Y (subtraction)

C=X×Y (multiplication)

D=X÷Y (division)

Now write down a single expression in BASIC which uses each of the values A, B, C, D once only, together with any of the following symbols:

+, (), −, ×, ÷

which will most nearly approximate to 27.38104965.

For example, suppose X=2 and Y=3.

Then:

A=5
B=−1
C=6 and
D=2÷3

then A×C+B÷D=28.5 which is getting close to the required answer − but we're sure you can do better.

45 Palindromic cycles

That title sounds like a bike with a saddle at both ends.

If any two-digit number is reversed and added to itself, and the process repeated over and over, eventually a palindromic number will result (i.e. one which reads the same forwards as backwards).

Thus, consider the number 19. When reversed it gives 91. Then 19+91=110.

And repeating, 110+011=121, which is palindromic after only two operations.

Which two-digit number requires the most number of operations before a palindromic sum is reached? And how many are required?

Clearly there will be two answers – since one will be the reverse of the other. Either one is acceptable.

46 Mother and daughter

A puzzle in logical deduction, with a bit of indeterminate algebra thrown in for good measure.

Four ladies went into a post office to buy stamps.

(1) Alice bought only 3p stamps.
Betty bought only 4p stamps.
Celia bought only 6p stamps.
Doris bought only 8p stamps
(2) The total money spent by the ladies was £1.61.
(3) The daughter got the fewest number of stamps and spent 24p.
(4) The mother got the most stamps and spent 72p.

Which of the four women were mother and daughter?

47 A catastrophic puzzle

A problem to bring out the Venn diagrams.

In my house there are many cats:

(1) Seven of the cats won't eat fish.
(2) Six of them won't eat liver.
(3) Five of them won't eat chicken.
(4) Four of them eat neither fish nor liver.
(5) Three of them eat neither fish nor chicken.
(6) Two of them eat neither liver nor chicken.
(7) One of them eats neither fish, liver, nor chicken.
(8) None of them eat all three foods.

How many cats have I got?

48 Susan's perfect man

Another puzzle in logic, but a little bit harder than the last one.

Susan's perfect man has black hair, brown eyes, and is tall and slim.

Susan knows four men – Arthur, Bill, Charles, and Dave. Only one of them has all the characteristics that Susan requires.

(1) Arthur and Bill have the same colour eyes.
(2) Only one of the men has both black hair and brown eyes.
(3) Bill and Charles have the same colour hair.
(4) Only two of the men are both tall and slim.
(5) Charles and Dave are of differing build.
(6) Only two of the men are both tall and dark-haired.
(7) Dave and Arthur are the same height.
(8) Only three of the men are both slim and brown-eyed.

Which is Susan's perfect man?

49 An interesting pair of series

Alas, no prizes for this one, but I hope it gives you a bit of pleasure.

You are given the two independent series shown – the terms in each are in ascending order of value.

Series A
1, 3, 8, A4, A5, A6, etc.

Series B
8, B2, 190, B4, B5, B6, etc.

In either series, the product of any two terms plus one gives a perfect square. Thus, in series A,

$1 \times 3 + 1 = 4$
$1 \times 8 + 1 = 9$
$3 \times 8 + 1 = 25$

Similarly in series B.

What you have to do is to find the values of B2, B4, and A4. To make things a bit easier, I can tell you that B2 and A4 both happen to have the same value.

By the way, if anyone comes up with a value for A5 or B5, would you please drop me a line – I don't have those solutions yet.

50 Another pyramid problem

A certain tetrahedral pyramid, i.e. one in which each layer is a triangle, is constructed from ball-bearings so that on the top there is one ball resting on three, and so on. The total number of balls in the pyramid is an exact square.

Assuming that there are at least three layers, how many are there – and how many ball-bearings?

51 A number and its square

Arrange the digits 1–9 inclusive so as to form two numbers, one of which is the square of the other.

There are two possible solutions – can you find them both?

52 A long-winded fraction

Can you find a fraction which has a six-digit number in the numerator, and a six-digit number in the denominator, and which, if you 'cancel' digits which appear in both numerator and denominator, gives the original value?

To illustrate, suppose the fraction is 123456/234567.

Then if we 'cancel' the digits 2, 3, 4, 5, and 6 from top and bottom, we are left with 1/7, but unfortunately this is not the value of the original fraction.

There are at least two solutions to the problem.

53 An infernal triangle

This problem is not one for micros, but it is such a diabolical teaser that I thought I should include it in this book. There are one or two other puzzles in this category elsewhere within these pages, but I think this is my all-time favourite.

I first encountered this puzzle about (dare I say it) thirty years ago while at university. I managed to find a solution (with the help of one of the maths professors), but it wasn't a very elegant one. Since that time, however, I have passed the puzzle around on many occasions, and acquired about three or four solutions, one of which you will find in the back of this book. I am reluctant to include the solution, since many people will not get the maximum pleasure from the problem, but will merely give up after half an hour and turn to the back pages. They will have deprived themselves of a lot of fun if they do.

So, here goes – make a resolve not to give in too soon.

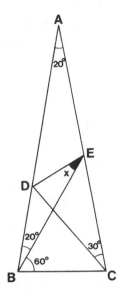

You are given the triangle shown, with the angles as marked. You are required to calculate the angle X – *but* you may use only methods of pure geometry, i.e. no trigonometry, no measuring permitted, merely Euclidean stuff.

54 The ladder and the wall

This is not strictly a non-micro problem, since you are likely to need the computer for the final bit, although it can be obviated as you will see from the solution.

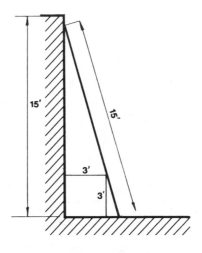

A ladder, 15 ft long, leans against a vertical wall 15 ft high. The ladder leans at such an angle that it just touches a 3 ft cubic box placed between the ladder and the wall as shown in the diagram.

How far from the top of the wall is the top of the ladder?

55 More ladders and walls

This ladder and wall problem is also one of my favourites. You may require the micro to solve the equations, but I advise you now that with a little bit of thought, that can be avoided.

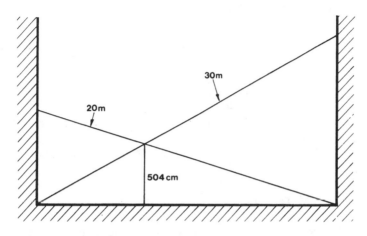

There are two vertical walls less than 25 metres apart. Two ladders, one of length 30 metres, and the other of length 25 metres (big ladders, eh?), rest against opposite walls as shown, and intersect exactly 504 cm above the ground.

How far apart are the walls?

56 Reflections at a corner

This puzzle is not a pure micro problem, nor is it too difficult, but I'm including it because of the neatness of solution.

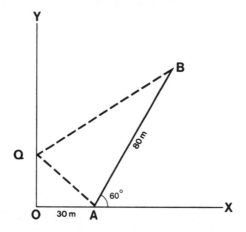

Two walls OX and OY intersect at right angles at the point O. Point A is 30 metres from this intersection along the wall OX, and point B is exactly 80 metres from A along a line AB drawn at an angle of 60° to the wall OX.

How far from O should a point Q be along the wall OY, so that the total distance AQ+QB is a minimum, i.e. what is the distance OQ?

57 The census taker

A lady census taker rings the doorbell of a house in a suburban street and a man comes to the door.

'Excuse me, sir,' says the census taker. 'Could you tell me how many people live here and what are their ages?'

'Certainly,' replies the man. 'But since you're obviously very interested in numbers, I'll let you work it out for yourself. There are three people living here. The product of their ages is 1296, and the sum of their ages is equal to the door number.'

The census taker smiles, and steps back to look at the door number, and the man adds:

'You'll also need to know that one of us here is as old as the total number of cars that you can see on this street.'

The census taker counts the number of cars that she sees, and then writes down the ages of the three occupants.

Assuming all ages are in whole numbers of years, what was the door number?

58　A number crossword

Capital letters refer to clues across. Lower-case letters refer to clues down.

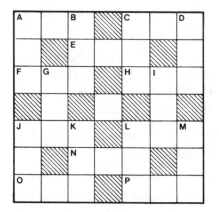

(A) Sum of digits=26.
(C) See g.
(E) (A+a)/3.
(F) Sum of digits=2.
(H) A square
(J) Sum of digits=11.
(L) E−C.
(N) (m−g)×4.
(O) See g.
(P) A−80.

(a) A square with sum of digits=16.
(b) Divisible by 60.
(c) Sum of digits=5.
(d) A square.
(g) $g^2+C^2=O^2$.
(i) d−H.
(j) a−300.
(k) Sum of digits=12.
(l) A square.
(m) E−H.

Sum of all digits is divisible by 29.

59 Another number crossword

Capital letters refer to clues across. Lower-case letters refer to clues down.

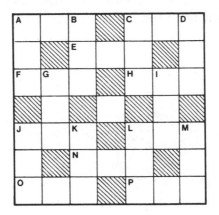

$A^2+C^2=d^2$.

$N^2+H^2=m^2$.

$I^2-a^2=b^2-j^2=120^2$.

$H=5\times m/13$.

$P=d-10=j-100$.

g is a square $+14$.

E is divisible by 10.

O is twice a prime.

$E=g/3$.

$L=p+8$.

$g=f\times k+10$.

$a=2\times c-8$.

$b=d+100$.

g's digits add up to 15.

$i=A-m$.

Sum of all digits is divisible by 19.

60 A series of primes

Very short and sweet, this one.

I want you to find the least number of consecutive prime numbers that add up to 106,620.

That's all.

61 The hymn board

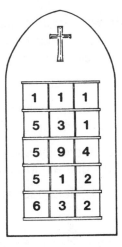

Several times during the long boring sermon, J. J. Clessa was tempted to close his eyes and doze, but he was afraid to do so in case he snored and drew attention to himself.

So he exercised his mind by looking at the numbers on the hymn board. There were five three-digit numbers as shown, but as J. J. realised, they could also be construed as three five-digit numbers by reading the board downwards instead of across.

In fact, he further calculated that if he divided each of the three five-digit numbers by his house number, he always got a remainder which was equal to the door number of his brother's house.

What is Clessa's house number?

62 Three unusual digits

The problem is to find three different digits such that, in whatever order they are used to make a three-digit number, that number will **not** be divisible by:

3, 5, 7, 11, 13, or 17

Furthermore, since more than one solution is possible, we are looking for the three digits whose product is the greatest.

To ensure that there is no ambiguity, suppose the three digits are a, b, and c. Then, none of the numbers:

abc, acb, bac, bca, cab, and cba

will divide by 3, 5, 7, 11, 13, or 17,

and also the product of a × b × c must be as large as possible.

63 A recurring quotient

This problem should get the PCs spinning. I don't think there's any other way to do it.

You have to find the most frequently recurring quotient that results when a five-digit number divides exactly by the sum of its digits.

For example, 82030 divides exactly by 13, which is the sum of its digits (8+2+0+3+0) to give a quotient of 6310.

63100 also divides exactly by 10 to give the same quotient— 6310.

What is the quotient that most frequently occurs?

64 A rotating grid

In the grid shown, the digits 1–9 are arranged so that the first row added to the second row equals the bottom row—583 + 146 = 729.

Now if the grid is rotated clockwise through 90°, you will see that the first two rows still add up to the last row—715 + 248 = 963.

Can you find another combination of the digits 1–9 which has the same property?

5	8	3
1	4	6
7	2	9

65 The cocktail party

A fairly simple puzzle in logic this time.

Six people meet at a cocktail party. Their names are Annie, Brian, Celia, Don, Erica, and Frank, and their professions, though not necessarily respectively, are Teacher, Engineer, Programmer, Doctor, Accountant, and Solicitor.

1. Frank and the Teacher both vote Tory.
2. Don and the Engineer both vote Liberal.
3. Annie and the Programmer both vote Labour.
4. Celia and Erica are both Scots. The programmer is Welsh.
5. The Accountant is older than Frank.
6. The Solicitor is older than Annie.
7. Celia and the Teacher both adore classical music.
8. Annie and the Accountant both hate the classics but love jazz.

What is each person's respective profession?

Answers

Quickies

1 81.

2 There is no missing £1. The dilemma is merely in the way in which the problem is posed. Each man paid £9, making £27 – of this, the waiter got £2 and the manager £25.

3 Statement (4), i.e. only four of the statements are false.

4 5.

5 A 5p piece and a 50p piece. We did say that one of them wasn't a 50p piece – but the other one is!

6

P	U	N	C	H
P	U	N	C	H
P	U	N	C	H
P	U	N	C	H
P	U	N	C	H

7 Three boys and four girls.

8 They are both the same distance away when they pass.

9 It would be you!

10 A bit naughty this one. He was smoking fifty a day at the outset, but he also had four cigarettes left over from his last packet.

11 Twenty-one pounds.

12 Each person gets one orange but one man also gets the box.

13 Twenty days.

14 Three ducks.

15 A day and a half.

16 IF=41. AT=35. FIAT=1435.

17 13.

18 12⅔.

19 2⅖.

20 There are approx. 1,094 million sq yd in a square metre and 1,609 million mm in a mile. Hence the answer is (b).

21 61. Each is a perfect square read from back to front.

22 The letters of NEW DOOR can easily be rearranged to form ONE WORD.

23 Since the relative speed of the trains to each other is 50+70=120 mph, i.e. 2 miles per minute, it follows that 15 minutes before crossing they will be 30 miles apart.

24 504.

25 Agreed. When written down the number is 12111.

26 The word INCORRECTLY. Amusingly enough, when this quickie first appeared, the editor of *PCW* at that time (who shall be nameless!) thought he would do a bit of editing and without realising the significance of the wording, changed it to:

'There is one word on this page which is not spelt correctly . . . !'

Which was the way in which it was first published.

27 He was standing 20 yards inside a tunnel.

28 Alan has three, Billy has six, and Charlie has eleven.

29 By the end of the 17th day and night he would be 3 feet from the top, and therefore on the 18th day, i.e. 18th February, he would climb 3 feet and reach the top.

30 7600 lb. There are four faces to the clock.

31 He would have to drive at infinite speed, therefore the answer is impossible. If you require further explanation, suppose the distance is 30 miles. Then it would take him one hour to get to work. Since the total journey is 60 miles, in order to average 60 mph, he would need to return home in no time at all.

32 The 50p didn't go anywhere. The figures are correct as they are. The apparent anomaly is caused by trying to add rates together to give an aggregate rate, i.e. so much per something, in our case pounds of tomatoes per 50p. You just can't do that and get the right answer. If the two ladies had wanted to fix a correct joint price, they would have had to calculate the price per pound in each case and then add them together. In this case it would have resulted in 50/3p per lb plus 50/2p per lb=41⅔p per 2 lb, or 6 lb for £1.25. There would then be no anomaly.

33 Easy. Just go vertically downwards to get to the land!

34 There are several ways of doing this. Here's a sample:

$$\frac{5+5}{5+5} = 1 \qquad\qquad \frac{55}{5} - 5 = 6$$

$$\frac{5}{5} + \frac{5}{5} = 2 \qquad\qquad \frac{5}{\cdot5} - \sqrt{\frac{5}{\cdot5}} = 7$$

$$\frac{5+5+5}{5} = 3 \qquad\qquad \frac{5}{\cdot5} - \frac{5}{5} = 8$$

$$5 - \frac{5}{\sqrt{5\times5}} = 4 \qquad\qquad \frac{5+5-5}{5} = 9$$

$$\frac{5\times5}{\sqrt{5\times5}} = 5 \qquad\qquad \frac{5}{\cdot5} - \frac{5}{5} = 10$$

35 The floor is six foot one inch below the egg.

36 You can't dig half a hole.

37 Rowing and backstroke swimming.

38 It contains the digits zero to nine in alphabetical order.

39 This is almost the same problem as Quickie 32. You can't add rates to get a total rate. For further explanation see the solution to Quickie 32.

40 Are you sitting comfortably? The rice paper would be 17,769,885 miles thick. If you don't believe it, try folding it yourself!

41 This is an old chestnut which my father (God rest his soul) first told to me. The standard answer is that they both weigh the same, since a pound is a pound, no matter what the material. But, in fact, feathers are measured on the Avoirdupois scale of weights in which there are 16 ounces to the pound, whereas gold is measured on the Troy scale in which there are 12 ounces to the pound. So the feathers would weigh the most.

42 This is the reason why Archimedes ran naked down the street crying, 'I've found it!' The water level would go up more if you put the penny into the saucer.

43 23 – the series is that of prime numbers.

44

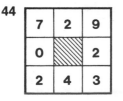

45 T – they are all letters composed of straight lines.

46 There are an infinite number of places where this could occur. The most obvious of these is the South Pole, but he could also be at any place which is 1 mile south of a point where the cross-section of the Earth is a circle of circumference 1 mile.

47 All births are of babies, not women.

48

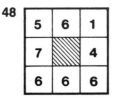

49 N – the series is one, two, three, four, etc.

50 500 – they are the units of UK currency.

51 31 and 10,000. Each term in the series is 16 expressed in a different number base starting with base 16.

52 Zero.

53 This is one of several solutions.

2	9	4
7	5	3
6	1	8

54 STARTLING
STARTING
STARING
STRING
STING
SING
SIN
IN
I

55 90.

56 West. Check it on the map if you don't believe it.

57 'I do.'

58 2½ pence.

59 47, 53, 59, 61.

60 Ninety games – since there will be ninety teams eliminated.

61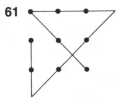

62 All the children are boys!

63 She had triplets.

64 Still only one rung, since the ship goes up with the water.

65 It was his mother.

66 Fifteen. First he smoked the ten, giving him ten butts. The he made three more from nine of the butts and had a butt left over. When he'd smoked those, he still had four butts, which made one more cigarette, and left him with two butts.

Then a friend came along and lent him a butt which he used to make his fifteenth cigarette, and when he'd smoked that he gave his friend his butt back.

67 The grandfather is his mother's father.

68 Half way, after that he's running out again.

69 The neighbouring farmer brings a cow to make the total 18.
He then gives the eldest son one-half – i.e. 9 cows.
He then gives the second son one-third – i.e. 6 cows.
He then gives his youngest son one-ninth – i.e. 2 cows,
making a total of 17 cows. So he then takes his own cow home.

70 His friends subscribe and buy him one.

Micropuzzles

1 Pythogoras for beginners

This problem is easily solved by heuristic methods (trial and error!), using a couple of nested loops in a BASIC computer program. The triangle with the smallest area is one with sides 144, 192, and 240. It has a perimeter of 144 and an area of 13,824.

2 Flying the Glasgow shuttle

This problem in logical reasoning should not have proved too difficult. The pilot's name is Smith.

3 A Chessboard dilemma

Hardly a problem for the micro – much more easily solved with a diagram and a few counters. There are two possible solutions, as shown.

4 A palindromic puzzle

This was a certainty for the micro – all you needed was a subroutine that would check for a number being palindromic. The following BASIC statements would do just that.

```
10   M0% = 0 : X$ = str$(X)
20   if left$(X$,1) = " " then X$ = mid$(X$,2) : goto 20
30   for I% = 1 to len(X$)/2
40      if mid$(X$,I%,1) <> mid$(X$,len(X$)+1−I%,1) then M0% = 1
50   next I%
60   return
```

Enter the subroutine with the number in double precision form in X. If the number is palindromic, the variable M0% will be zero on exit.

For the discerning reader, line 20 removes leading spaces which some BASICs add when they convert a number to string format.

Once you have this, or a similar routine, then the problem can be easily solved by a simple loop program, although if you wished, you could find ways of speeding up the calculation.

The answers are as follows:

(1) Alan's and Bert's mileometers are palindromic again after 321123 miles.
(2) Alan's and Colin's mileometers are palindromic again after 111111 miles.
(3) Bert's and Colin's mileometers are palindromic again after 0110 miles.
(4) All three mileometers are mutually palindromic after 655666 miles.

5 Digital dexterity

This isn't really one for the micros, unless of course, you have a routine for dealing with very large integers – i.e. multiple precision. Subroutines can be written without too much difficulty for this purpose – some systems have them supplied.

Analytically, however, the problem can be solved as follows:

Consider the number in the form
$$X=A0+10 \times A1+100 \times A2+1000 \times A3+. \text{ etc} \dots +10^n \times An$$

Then, the required condition is satisfied if

$$A0 \times X=A1+10 \times A2+100 \times A3 +\dots +10^{n-1} \times An+10 \times A0$$

i.e. $$X=\frac{A0(10^{n+1}-1)}{10 \times A0-1}$$

Therefore $\dfrac{10^{n+1}-1}{10 \times A0-1}$ must be integral.

Hence, to find the solution for $A0-2$, the denominator of the above fraction is 19, therefore we must find a power of 10 which is one more than a multiple of 19. The smallest is 10 to the power of 19, which is 1 followed by 18 zeros. The required value of X can then be calculated longhand very simply, albeit laboriously.

The solutions to the puzzle are:

(2) 105, 263, 157, 894, 736, 842
(3) 1,034, 482, 758, 620, 689, 655, 172, 413, 793
(4) 102564
(5) 102, 040, 816, 326, 530, 612, 244, 897, 959, 183, 673, 469, 387, 755
(6) 1,016, 949, 152, 542, 372, 881, 355, 932, 203, 389, 830, 508, 474, 576, 271, 186, 440, 677, 966
(7) 1,014, 492, 753, 623, 188, 405, 797
(8) 1,012, 658, 227, 848
(9) 10,112, 359, 550, 561, 797, 752, 808, 988, 764, 044, 943, 820, 224, 719

Phew!

6 A palindromic square

No problems here, if you use the subroutine that we described in the solution to Micropuzzle 4. The answer is 698896, which is the square of 836.

7 More perfect squares

When this puzzle was originally set, we were surprised to find quite a large percentage of entrants who got it wrong. Again, it shouldn't have been too difficult to write a small program to solve it – probably consisting of three nested loops.

As it turns out, the smallest answer could have been calculated quite easily with pencil and paper. 25 is the average of 1 and 49.

8 A question of logic

This was a puzzle in logical thought. The correct answer was GREEN. The solution could be deduced by trial and error, testing each colour possibility in turn and eliminating ones which proved invalid.

9 The whole truth and nothing but the truth

Another logical puzzle. There was a lovely rhyme about this from a reader in Edinburgh which I must include here.

I slowly strolled beside the sea,
And chanced upon some natives three,
With natives evenly divided
Twixt truth, untruth, and undecided.

I asked of one which tribe was he,
And which were numbers two and three,
He mumbled first then spoke outright,
The first one's grey, two's black, three's white.

I pondered this reply untrue
(White could not be both three and two),
Until at last it dawned on me,
They were black – one, white – two, grey – three.

You can't put the answer better than that!

10 Talking turkey

A nice problem for a micro. A simple counter is needed to keep tabs on the number of days in the month, but otherwise straightforward enough.

The answers are:

Last bird eaten is no. 63.
Christmas dinner 1985 is no. 76.

11 The not-so-perfect square

This puzzle proved to be a real toughie! Many readers swore that it was impossible (I'll bet many of you have reached that conclusion too). Some just swore! That was because they were thinking in integers and not considering the possibility that fractions can be perfect squares too.

The answer is $(41/12)^2$.

If you add 5 you get $(49/12)^2$.

If you subtract 5 you get $(31/12)^2$.

12 Squaring the cube

This was a bit more difficult than usual. But it succumbs to computer solution if you tackle it correctly. If you merely generate all possibilities one by one, you could end up taking literally years.

A bit of thought, however, will tell you one number must contain six digits and the other four digits. 3 and 7 or 5 and 5 are not possible.

If you also realise that since all squares end in either 0, 1, 4, 5, 6, or 9, then the four-digit number cannot end in 2, 3, 7, or 8, otherwise its cube could not be a square. Furthermore, since any digit can only be used once only, numbers ending in 0 or 5 are eliminated also. This means that the four-digit number must end in 1, 4, 6, or 9.

You can now write a simple loop to try all possibilities that are left. You will still need a subroutine which will tell you if the digits are used only once, but that can be overcome with a table look-up approach with the numbers converted to string form.

The answer is 4761 and 328509.

13 A natural mistake

The problem can be easily solved by micro since the range of numbers isn't too great. When we set it, we hadn't considered the possibility of using a one-half pence coin, so there were answers that we hadn't allowed for.

There are three solutions:

(1) £1.20, £1.25, £1.50, £3.16.
(2) £1.12½, £1.28, £1.58, £3.12½.
(3) £1.18½, £1.20, £1.60, £3.12½.

14 Ten-digit perfect square

Not too difficult for a micro provided you have double precision arithmetic facilities. If not then you'd better write your own, for many of these puzzles require numbers larger than those which most standard BASICs will handle. It shouldn't be too difficult if you use two or more integer variables in array form to represent the parts of each number.

In addition you'll need the facility for counting digits used, but this would be similar to the routine that was needed for solving Micropuzzle 12.

The ten answers are as follows:

(0) 1,600,000,000.
(1) 1,101,111,489.
(2) 1,254,222,225.
(3) 3,333,330,225.
(4) 4,434,494,464.
(5) 4,555,575,025.
(6) 4,666,665,969.
(7) 7,907,477,776.
(8) 3,828,886,884.
(9) 2,909,199,969.

15 A bad connection

When this puzzle was first set in *PCW*, the 14p stamp was just being introduced. In fact, one reader said the problem was impossible, because it hadn't, up to then. I wonder if you will still be able to buy 14p stamps when this book is published.

Incidentally, I wonder if the Post Office do withdraw stamps from circulation any time. It would be hard to see how they could, since there'd be bound to be someone who kept some. I suppose that must mean that stamps can't be treated like coins – e.g. withdrawn from circulation – or can they?

Anyway, the puzzle was a problem in logic. If you consider all possible ways in which you can spend the £2 on the particular stamps, buying at least one of each, which is what the first sentence in the conversation implies, then there are five possibilities, as shown:

	12p	14p	17p	Total
(1)	8	5	2	15
(2)	1	11	2	14
(3)	4	6	4	14
(4)	7	1	6	14
(5)	3	2	8	13

Since the total number of stamps wasn't enough to tell B the numbers of each that had been bought, we can eliminate (1) and (5) from the list. So there must have been fourteen stamps.

Now if the answer to the question 'Did you buy only one of one kind . . . had been 'Yes', then there still would not have been sufficient information, since cases (2) and (4) both contain one of one kind. Therefore the answer to the question must have been 'No', and hence B was able to say, 'In that case, you bought . . .' So that means that case (3) was the one.

The answer therefore is:

4×12p stamps
6×14p stamps
4×17p stamps

16 A numerical traverse

This problem could be solved by micro, since the number of combinations of moves isn't too enormous (each move opens up three possible moves), but in fact it probably was just as easy to find the answer by pencil and paper, which is what most contestants did.

The two routes giving maximum difference were:

(1) Start-8-14-8-18-14-19-16-18-15-17-Finish (166).
(2) Start-2-2-3-3-7-11-2-2-1-1-8-Finish (42).

Giving a difference of 124.

17 A problem of check-digits

This is a nice little micro application, which involves not just the usual number-bashing, but requires a little bit of sophisticated programming if done properly. In particular, the routine to generate possible weights which are multiples of successive primes would be interesting to program. However, you could be lazy and leave a six-level nested loop running for a week or two, if you wished.

Anyway, however you tackled the problem, you will have the correct answer if the weights you obtained were:

82, 86, 94, 53, 59, 61, respectively,

and the check-sum of the ninth number is 51.

18 Ceremonial rice pudding

This puzzle caused quite a few sarcastic comments about the length of time that the poor of the village had to wait before they got fed. It was an ideal problem for the number-bash type of approach that is so easy using a micro program. It can be reduced a bit if you consider only situations when the total number of grains to date divides exactly by 23.

Since the number of grains after n hours is

$$n \times (1+n)/2$$

then for this to divide by 23, clearly n would need to be a multiple of 22 or 23. This will eliminate much of the search.

The answer is that each villager gets 3,218,436 grains, if he hasn't starved to death before then, since the ceremony lasts for 12,167 hours, which is just over a year!

19 Who's who

Another puzzle in logical reasoning, easily solved with a grid in which the rows are used for the vocations, and the columns for names.

Mr Baker turns out to be the parson.

20 Word frustration

This puzzle is ideal for micros, but not for calculators without alpha facility. the way to approach this is to write a program which generates all possible combinations of moves, starting with a one-character string, then forming four two-character strings, and displaying the strings on the screen.

If any string makes alphabetical sense (i.e. a possible word), then its four derivatives should be generated and also displayed. (You will need to store valid strings in an array as they are built up.) If the string clearly has a non-permissible sequence of letters (this approach would be impossible in Poland!), then it need not be developed further. As the program proceeds, you will eliminate all but the correct solution, although your eyes will probably be watering by the time you've finished.

If you do this correctly, you will come up with the correct sequence of words, which was:

DEBATES
ORATORY
UNDYING
BARTERS
LASTING
EASTERN
STERNLY

Making the required word DOUBLES.

21 A positional problem

I suppose this puzzle can be solved only by trial and error, but for that purpose the micro could be useful. The problem is very similar to the well-known chess problem where you must put eight queens on a chessboard so that no queen can be taken by any other.

To generate the possible solutions by micro would call for an initial definition for each position (1 to 64) of the other positions which were on the same diagonal. Then, if you initially set up an array with sixty-four elements set to zero, you could allocate the first square to the first queen, and set the values of all other 'takeable' squares to 1. Then search down the array for the next zero element and repeat. Once a solution had been found, you could flag the squares used in some way so as to avoid its repetition.

Anyway, that should give you an idea for a computer approach. Once you had obtained a combination, you could then easily evaluate its score – and so obtain the maximum.

Incidentally, that maximum is 62, obtained from the squares A6, A7, B1, D2, F6, F7, G4, H1.

22 Generating a specific value

This puzzle shouldn't have proved too hard for a number-crunching solution – I don't know any other method by which you could have done it.

The values of X and Y to give the maximum value of E are 64321 and 5, respectively, giving E=19,856, 844,651.

23 Sums of squares

A rather tough one, this, and I can't see an algorithm that would be convenient for programming. Clearly, the more squares you can get from two integers, the better will be the score, and when there are no more two-integer squares, then three-integer squares are the next best. On the other hand, it is essential to use all the integers, so, all in all, I'm pleased that I just set the puzzles, and don't always have to solve them!

Anyway, the maximum score that was submitted (by about seventeen entrants) was 97 obtained as follows (/ separates the squares, and a comma separates the integers comprising the squares):

1,3 / 4,5 / 2,6,8 / 12,13 / 16,20 / 31,33 / 40,41 / 9,10,23,26,32 /
25,27,34,35 / 19,36,37,38,39 / 29,30,42,47,48 /
11,14,15,17,18,22,24,44,60 / 21,28,45,46,52,64 / 7,49,51,53,63,66 /
50,67,68,69,70 / 56,58,59,61,62,65 / 54,55,57,77,78,79, /
43,71,72,73,74,75,76

This solution uses all the integers.

24 A very prime word

It's strange how an alphabetic puzzle can be guaranteed to produce a low response from *PCW* readers. I've never understood why, but it's definitely so. I would have thought that all you computer whizzes would have been into crosswords and any kind of puzzle, and not just the numeric ones. Perhaps it's because you can't get the computer to help so easily.

Anyway, with this puzzle, I would have thought that you could generate primes and translate them into words and print them out. There may be too many for the average micro, but I happen to know that one or two of my readers are not averse to using any computer power available – the more the better – and quite a few mainframes have been known to have expended the odd second or two on *PCW* 'Leisure Lines' problems!

The best solution submitted was made up of the prime number 2,772,776,528,653 which translates to ASSASSINATING.

25 Fieldcraft

If you attempt to solve this problem by a computer program, you should consider the horizontal side of the field to be split into intervals of, say, 100×6 ft. Then set up an equation (using Pythagoras) for the distance and thence derive the travel time between one of the intervals on AD and another on EF, and similarly the distance and travel time between the intervals on EF and GH, and GH and BC.

Then the problem can be solved by a program with four nested loops which vary the intervals on AD from 1 to 100, and then on EF from the AD value to 100, and then on GH from the EF value of 100, and finally on BC from the GH value to 100. (I hope you can understand that.)

When you have obtained the 6 ft intervals within which the minimum time occurs, then you can break these sections into say seventy-two one-inch intervals, and repeat the process, down to any level of accuracy that you require – although to the nearest inch is probably good enough.

The answer you should get is 2 minutes and 22 seconds.

26 Opening day at the school

A logical puzzle, which had an ambiguity in its original wording, but which we have now removed. So, you should therefore have reached a single solution, which is TUESDAY.

27 A very charitable dilemma

Another logical problem, and I'm afraid I know of no easy way of solving this other than by generating all the money distribution combinations – either manually, or by means of a computer program.

The answer is that there are fifty relatives and six charities.

28 Cows, pigs, and horses

More logic. Again no explanation is needed other than the hint to think at the outset of which pens could contain horses. This gives us a set of possibilities such that pens C, D, or F can contain horses, and if there is more than one horse, there must be two only, in pens C and F.

From this you can deduce that the animals are as follows:

Sheep in C.
Pigs in A, F, H.
Cows in B, E, G.
Horse in D.

29 An exact number of factors

Although this problem can be 'bashed out' fairly easily with a little bit of programming, it can also be solved analytically.

Suppose the number that we are seeking is A. Then suppose its prime factors are P1, P2, P3, etc.

Now, if we express A in terms of powers of these prime factors

$A = P1^a \times P2^b \times P3^c \times \ldots$

then the number A will contain exactly $(a+1) \times (b+1) \times (c+1) \ldots$ factors including unity and the number itself.

Now since we want a number which will contain 104 factors excluding unity, i.e. 105 including unity, and also since $105 = 3 \times 5 \times 7$, we can choose any three prime factors, P1, P2, and P3, and values of $a = 2$, $b = 4$, $c = 6$.

Then the product of $P1^2 \times P2^4 \times P3^6$ will give us a number with exactly 104 factors, excluding unity.

In order to get the smallest number, we should choose P1, P2, and P3 accordingly – i.e. P1 = 2, P2 = 3, and P3 = 5. This gives a value A = 129,600.

Similarly, if we require the smallest odd number, then we must exclude 2 from our choice of prime factors. Then, the smallest possible result will be when P1 = 3, P2 = 5, P3 = 7, and the value obtained will be 22,325,625.

30 Cubes and squares

Very easy, this one. Ideal for a programming solution. All that is needed is to generate the cube and the fourth power of successive integers. Since 300 raised to the power of 4 is almost an eleven-digit number, you can see that you don't have to go too far in a loop. The only problem for the program is to test that all the digits 0–9 are used, and this is a recurring requirement in this type of problem, so by now, no doubt, you'll have a subroutine for doing just that.

The solution is that $x = 18$, and that the cube $= 5832$, and the fourth power $= 104976$.

31 A question of remainders

Another fairly easy one. Simple to program – even readily solvable on a programmable calculator. Not worth discussing further, except to give the two possible answers 5039 and 7559.

32 A problem of prime factors

This puzzle is more easily solved by analytical methods than by computing.

Let us suppose we start off by considering the worst possible case, where the factors are 97, 2, and 1. Now the number would be $97 \times 2 \times 1$.

Now if we replace the 97 by 89, 5 and 3, then clearly the product will increase. If we then exchange the 5 for a 3 and a 2, then the product will increase further. The only level at which it becomes disadvantageous to exchange one prime factor for two smaller ones is when the factors are 2s. The two 3s are preferable to three 2s.

And so the maximum product will be found when the factors are 2s and 3s, but with not more than two 2s. That is, when $X = 2^2 \times 3^{32}$, giving $X = 7,412,080,755,407,364$.

33 The ladies of the committee

A nice puzzle in logic, solvable with squared paper and a pencil for a change. The answer was summed up beautifully in rhyme by a reader from Scotland (as was an earlier puzzle – I thought it was the Welsh that were supposed to be the bards?).

When all the votes were counted,
And likes and dislikes reckoned,
The Captain's place went Audrey's way,
With Freda closely second.

Wee Betty was made Treasurer,
But what a fuss, I guess.
If that's what golfing folks are like,
I think I'll stick to chess.

34 An unusual number

Fairly straightforward number-crunching, although as usual, a bit of thought and planning in advance will cut down the processing time.

There were two solutions:

109989, which when multiplied by 9 gives 989901.
219978, which when multiplied by 4 gives 879912.

35 Tadpoles, terrapins, tortoises, and turtles

Can be done analytically – probably more quickly than by a micro program, but certainly the micro approach is on. I'll give the analytical method here so you'll get the idea for future puzzles if you're not familiar with the approach.

Let's suppose the numbers of tadpoles, terrapins, tortoises, and turtles are A, B, C, and D respectively.

Then we have two equations:

(1) $59A + 199B + 287C + 344D = 10000$ (pence).
(2) $A + B + C + D + 100$.

If we substitute for A from equation (2) into equation (1), we get:

(3) $140B + 228C + 285D = 4100$.

Dividing (3) by 140 (the least coefficient) gives:

(4) $B + C + 88C/140 + 2D + 5D/140 = 29 + 40/140$.

Since B, C, D are integers, it follows that

$$\frac{88C + 5D - 40}{140}$$

must be also integer, say M. Then, we have:

(5) $88C + 5D - 40 = 140M$

which we again divide by the smallest coefficient, in this case 5. This gives us:

(6) $17C + 3C/5 + D - 8 = 28M$.

Hence, $3C/5$ must be integer, therefore $C = 5, 10, 15$, etc. If $C = 5$, then $80 + D = 281$, and thus $D = 4$, or 32, or 60, etc. (All possible solutions can be followed up, but for this purpose, I shall merely use the obvious one.)

Thus, if $C = 5$, and $D = 4$, then equation (3) gives $B = 13$, and finally, equation (2) gives $A = 78$. Hence the required solution is that there are 78 tadpoles, 13 terrapins, 5 tortoises, and 4 turtles. This is the only solution in which all creatures are present, although there are other solutions in which only three out of the four are bought.

36 More cubes and squares

This is probably best approached by the old faithful method of number-bashing on the micro. On the other hand, it is a relatively simple task to set down the factors of 2,000,000 at the outset, and thus save a little bit of calculation. In fact, if you are lucky enough to possess a calculator which works to ten places, you will probably find the problem quite trivial.

The answer is 5000, since $300^3 - 2,000,000 = 5000^2$.

37 Sums of cubes

Another one for the micro. No explanation needed, I would think, except that you should start with successive integers, and for each different starting point, try, say, up to 100 consecutive cubes, testing the accumulated sum at each step to see if you have a perfect square.

If you haven't got the answer by the time your starting integer is 15, then your program has a bug in it, because the correct answer is 97344 which is the sum of twelve consecutive cubes starting at 14, i.e. $97344 = 312^2 = 14^3 + 15^3 + 16^3 + \ldots + 25^3$.

38 Coconuts galore

This is truly a golden oldie, a classic puzzle that appears in may shapes and guises. Although a micro could handle it by trial and error of successive values, there is a very neat analytical solution which I came across several years ago.

If there are m men, then clearly $1-m$ is a solution, albeit a negative one, since, if you take one away (the one for the monkey), and then divide the remainder by m, it will mean that each man gets -1. If one man then takes his portion and puts the rest back, then there will be $1-m$ again. And the process can be repeated.

Now, if there are m men, there will be $m+1$ share-outs, and therefore, besides $1-m$ being a solution, there will also be solutions at intervals of:

$1-m+m^{(m+1)}$ and
$1-m+2\times m^{(m+1)}$ and
$1-m+3\times m^{(m+1)}$

and at every multiple of $m^{(m+1)}$.

But clearly, the least positive solution will be $1-m+m^{(m+1)}$.

In our problem, m=6, therefore the minimum number of coconuts is:

$1-6+6^7=279,931$ coconuts.

39 More trouble with remainders

A simple computer solution, with a loop from 5,000 to 50,000, and several remainder tests within that loop. The process can be considerably speeded up if you make the increment within the loop equal to the largest of the divisors – in this case 17.

The rest is easy, and the answer that you should get is 29031.

40 Ball-bearing pyramids

The only hard part about this problem is in working out the formulae for the number of ball-bearings in n layers of each of the three types of pyramid.

This is as follows:

(1) The square pyramid

$A = n \times (n+1) \times (2n+1)/6$

(2) The triangular pyramid

$A = n \times (n+1) \times (n+2)/6$

(3) The rectangular pyramid with top layer of b balls

$A = n \times (n+1) \times (2n+3b-2)/6$

Using these formulae, you can work out the number of balls contained in any frustrum of the pyramid, between any two layers, and that is all you need for the solution.

If you use the micro for solving this problem, you will quickly prove that the only pyramid that can possibly contain 36894 balls is a rectangular one with top layer of 11, and 43 layers in all. The area of ground covered would be approx. 43×53 square inches – some pyramid!

41 Sums of primes, etc.

A little bit nastier than normal, this one, although the numbers involved
do not call for double precision work.

To tackle it by program would require you to set up an array for storing
all the prime numbers up to 8999 – there are approximately 1200 of
them. If you haven't enough storage for this, then you would need to
generate them each different number you test. The BASIC subroutine
shown below will generate successive primes for you, relatively
efficiently.

Once you have the primes, then all you need do is test each odd integer
between 1 and 8999 to meet the required criteria. This would entail
successive testing of each prime in the array to see whether the
difference between it and the odd integer was twice a perfect square.

There may be easier methods, but there's something very satisfying
about solving a problem by computer trial and error which you wouldn't
be able to solve analytically.

After all the processing has finished – and the above program will get
slower, as the integer being tested increases – you will find that there
are two answers, 5777 and 5993.

Now here's the subroutine which will generate successive primes
starting at 11. It uses a function FNDIV which you will need to define at
the start of your program. Also you will need to initialise the variable X
with a value of 9 and the variable Q1% with the value of 1.

If you should need to use this routine for other problems, and you would
wish to start generating primes from, say, 2000 onwards, then you
should set X to any number ending in 9, below the point where you wish
to start – in this case 1999 – and set Q1% to 1. (You may alternatively
set X to a number that ends with 1, 3, or 7; Q1% must then be
initialized to 2, 3, or 4, respectively.)

The subroutine is entered at line 100, and on exit the variable X
contains the next prime, and the routine is left (dare I say it?) primed for
the next value to be produced.

```
10   X = 9 : Q1% = 1 'initial values
20   def fndiv(I) = X − I * int(X/I)
```

```
100   on Q1% goto 110, 130, 150, 170
110   X = X+2 : Q1% = 2
111      for I = 3 to sqr(X) step 2
112         if fndiv(I) = Ø then 130
113      next I
114      goto 190
130   X = X+2 : Q1% = 3
131      for I = 3 to sqr(X) step 2
132         if fndiv(I) = Ø then 150
133      next I
134      goto 190
150   X = X+4 : Q1% = 4
151      for I = 3 to sqr(X) step 2
152         if fndiv(I) = Ø then 170
153      next I
154      goto 190
170   X = X+2 : Q1% = 1
171      for I = 3 to sqr(X) step 2
172         if fndiv(I) = Ø then 110
173      next I
174      goto 190
190   return
```

42 The numerate marathon runner

A fairly easy problem, and one which should have been a doddle for the home (or office) computer. However, instead of bashing it through from scratch, a little bit of initial analysis can save a lot of programming time.

If you know that the formula for the sum of n successive integers starting at 1 is given by:

$$sum = n \times (n+1)/2$$

then, if the runner is number X and there are Y runners,

(a) the sum of the numbers up to and including his is $(X+1) \times X/2$;
(b) the sum of all the numbers is $(Y+1) \times Y/2$.

Hence the sum of numbers above his must be (b)−(a) and the sum of numbers below his will equal (a)−X.

Since these two values are to be equal, we find that the equations simplify to: $2X^2 = Y^2 + Y = Y \times (Y+1)$.

So we have to find an integer which when multiplied by the next integer above gives twice a perfect square, and which lies between 100 and 1000 (since there are other solutions).

This is easily obtained by micro or pocket calculator, and the answer is that X=204 and Y=288.

43   Ten-digit primes

Not much sophistication about this problem. As far as I'm aware, the only way to solve it is by a hard slog on the micro. You could make use of the prime number generator routine described in the answer to Micropuzzle 41, but you will need to extend it to use double precision arithmetic.

Many of our intrepid readers got the correct answers when the puzzle was originally set, but as I remarked earlier, I have good reason to suppose that there is a correlation between the publication date of PCW and the peaking of main-frame usage throughout the country (and overseas too, I'll be bound).

The answers to this problem (ten parts) are:

0 – 1,000,000,007	5 – 5,555,555,557
1 – 1,111,111,121	6 – 6,666,666,661
2 – 2,222,222,291	7 – 7,777,717,777
3 – 3,333,133,333	8 – 8,888,880,881
4 – 4,444,444,447	9 – 9,199,999,999

44 Approximations

This requires a bit more effort than just the usual micro slog. I would tackle it by setting up as many as possible of the BASIC expressions using A, B, C, and D together with the limited arithmetic operators that are provided (at least, you don't have to consider roots, factorials, and such like). Naturally you will not cover all possibilities, since using brackets does enlarge the number of combinations, but some will obviously be unnecessary.

Then you can put program loops around these, to vary X and Y, between reasonable limits. When you see the direction that the results are taking, you can modify the loop values, and eliminate equations as you wish. That's how I would have tackled the problem – but then, I probably wouldn't have got the correct solution which was an exact one:

X=5,476,209,930   Y=20,000

The correct expression is (A+B)/(C÷D).

45 Palindromic cycles

Delightful problem for even the smallest of micros. You would need to use a routine for checking palindromicity(?), on the lines of the one I presented with an earlier puzzle.

Apart from that, you should have no difficulty in getting the correct solution, which was: 89, or 98.

Either of these becomes palindromic after 24 operations.

46 Mother and daughter

This one was a little bit tougher than usual, but examine the equation

$3A+4B+6C+8D=161$

(where A, B, C, and D are the numbers of stamps bought by Alice, Betty, Celia, and Doris, respectively).

This equation can be transposed to

$3(A+2C)+4(B+2D)=161$.

If we divide through by 3, we find that $B+2D-2$ must be divisible by 3.

This gives us a range of possibilities for B and D, remembering that the least value can be 3 and the maximum value 24.

If we write down these possibilities, and then look at the combinations available for A and C, the problem comes down to three possible solutions:

(1) A=11, B=8,   C=12, D=3.
(2) A=7,   B=11, C=12, D=3.
(3) A=11, B=18, C=4,   D=4.

However, solution (3) involves a tie for the fewest number of stamps, and the problem does state that the daughter bought the fewest number, so therefore we must assume that there was no tie.

Of the two remaining possible solutions, in both cases the outcome is the same – C is the mother, and D is the daughter.

47 A catastrophic puzzle

Not too difficult.

For those who don't know how to solve this type of problem, here's an explanation. First draw a Venn diagram. You do this by drawing a square to represent all cats, and then within it you can draw three intersecting circles – the circles representing the cats who eat fish, liver, and chicken, respectively.

Where two circles overlap is an area where both foods are eaten, and where all three circles overlap is where all three foods are eaten. Finally, the area outside the circles and within the square represents those cats who eat none of the foods.

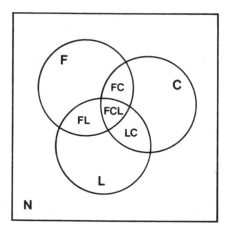

To make things clearer, we have marked the spaces in our diagram with letters:

FCL = All foods
N = None of the foods
F = Fish only
C = Chicken only
L = Liver only
FC = Fish and chicken (where F and C overlap)
FL = Fish and liver
CL = Chicken and liver

Now we are told that no cat eats all three foods, therefore we can put a zero in space FCL.

And since we know that one cat eats none of the foods, we can put a 1 in space N.

Because two cats eat neither liver nor chicken, then the number of cats in all spaces which don't contain an L or a C must be 2. There are two such spaces – N and F – and since N contains a 1, then F must also contain 1.

Now, three cats eat neither fish nor chicken, so the number of cats in spaces without a F or C must be 3. There are two such spaces – N and L, and since N contains a 1, L must be 2.

And so on. At the end, when you have gone through all the conditions, and all the areas are accounted for, you can count up just how many cats there are – and the answer is 10.

48 Susan's perfect man

This is another logical puzzle, slightly more difficult than most, but if you first build up a list of the attributes of each of the four men present without considering who has which, you will find that the men present comprise:

one who is tall, dark, slim, and brown-eyed;
one who is tall, not dark, slim and brown-eyed;
one who is tall, dark, not slim and not brown-eyed;
one who is not tall, dark, slim and brown-eyed.

At this point you can consider each of the possibilities in regard to how the four men fit the attributes. The only valid assignment is if Arthur is the ideal man.

49 An interesting pair of series

Although I am aware of an analytical solution to this problem, it is relatively easy to solve by brute force, using a simple computer program – at least, insofar as B2, A4, and B4 are concerned. Beyond that I'm afraid I don't have any answers, although since I first became aware of the problem, some twenty years ago, I have been told that either A5 or B5 must have in excess of 100 digits each. So I certainly would not want to have to check any answer that any reader sent in.

Anyway, B2=A4=120, and B4=730236.

50 Another pyramid problem

This puzzle is not too easy to solve by analysis, but before it can be solved by micro, you need to set up the equation for each successive row of balls. These would be:

1, 3, 6, 10, 15, 21, . . .
i.e. 1, 1+2, 1+2+3, 1+2+3+4, 1+2+3+4+5, etc.

and the nth layer would contain:

$1+2+3+4+5+ \ldots +n=(1+n) \times n/2$.

The sum of each successive layer can then be computed and accumulated without the need for further analysis, and the only possible solution in which this sum is a perfect square (apart from the case when there are just four ball-bearings) is when there are 48 layers.

This gives a total of 196,000 balls which is the square of 140.

51 A number and its square

This is a problem which requires a great deal of knowledge of number theory to solve by analytical means, and since this book is concerned with microcomputer methods, then that's the procedure we'd recommend.

Nevertheless, it is apparent that the number and its square must contain three and six digits respectively, since no two-digit number when squared give a seven-digit number. Similarly, no four-digit number squared gives a five-digit number.

Furthermore, since there is only one of each digit, the number cannot end in 1 or 5 or 6 (since its square would also then end in the same digit). If you think about the problem a bit, you can eliminate a lot of the permutations, but don't overdo the thought since the beauty of the micro solution is that it's easier to program the simple solution, even though the running time might be longer.

The simplest way, though probably not the fastest, is to generate all combinations of three-digit numbers using a simple loop, and to test the string value of the square of these for the necessary criteria.

Anyway, there are two possible solutions:

567 squared which equals 321,489.
854 squared which equals 729,316.

52 A long-winded fraction

There are two possible solutions,

$$\frac{166666}{666664} = \frac{1}{4} \quad \text{and} \quad \frac{199999}{999995} = \frac{1}{5}$$

In fact, you can add as many 6s to top and bottom of the first fraction, or 9s to the second fraction without changing the result, providing you keep the same number of digits in both numerator and denominator.

53 The infernal triangle

The answer is that X=30°. But if you measured it first and then managed to prove that it was 30°, then you are disqualified, even though that would be difficult enough.

The most elegant proof that we know goes as follows:

(1) Draw an arc about B with radius BE to cut AB and F and BC produced at G. Join EG and EF.
(2) △ AEB and △BDC are both isosceles. Therefore AE=EB and BD=BC.
(3) △BEG is equilateral and △BEF is isosceles since BF=BE=BG.
(4) Hence △AFE=△ECG, since
AE=BE=EG
$\angle$FAE=$\angle$CEG=20°
$\angle$AFE=$\angle$ECG=100°
Therefore, EF=CG.
(5) Now BF=BG and BD=BC, therefore FD=CG, and hence FD=FE.
(6) Thus DEF is isosceles, and $\angle$FDE=$\angle$FED=50°.
Therefore angle X=80°−50°=30°.

54 The ladder and the wall

At first sight, this problem leaves you with a quartic equation needing solution, which of course, if you know how, can easily be handled by those of you with micros.

However, a simple substitution trick can avoid this need and you will only have to handle a quadratic equation, which of course, can be solved by formula.

Let the distance from floor to top of ladder be x ft.
Let the distance from wall to bottom of ladder be y ft.

Then, the two basic equations for these two variables are obtained by Pythagoras, and similar triangles, respectively.

(1)   x+y=225

(2) $\dfrac{(x-3)}{3} = \dfrac{3}{(y-3)}$

Equation (2) simplifies to $3(x+y)=xy$.
Equation (1) can be transformed into $(x+y) -2xy=225$.

At this point, if we substitute p for $(x+y)$, and q for xy, we can obtain a quadratic equation in p or q, allowing us to calculate first p and q, and then by back-substitution x and y.

The two possible solutions (since x and y are interchangeable) are 14.5155 and 3.7810.

55 More ladders and walls

Again, as with the earlier ladder problem, at first sight we have here another formidable quartic equation to solve presumably by brute-force computing methods. Well, if you did the problem that way, fine – it shows that you are making good use of your micro – but, as you will see, the problem can also be solved more elegantly than that.

From the original diagram the following pair of equations can be readily obtained (pythagoras and similar triangles).

(1) $30-a^2=25-b^2$

(2) $\dfrac{1}{a} \dfrac{1}{b} = \dfrac{1}{h}$

Equation (1) simplifies to $(a-b) (a+b) = 25\times11$.
Equation (2) simplifies to $\dfrac{(a+b)}{ab} = \dfrac{25}{126}$

Now, if we make use of the fact that the ladders intersect *exactly* 504 cm above the ground, this implies that irrational solutions are to be avoided, and a closer examination of the two equations above will reveal that $a=18$ and $b=7$ satisfy the requirements.

These values, in turn, give the distance between the ladders as 24 metres.

56 Reflections at a corner

As we said, the beauty of this problem is in the simple method of solution, and the title of the puzzle should have provided a fair clue as to this method.

The problem can be solved from start to finish by trigonometry and calculus, but it is so much easier if you consider the concept of light reflecting from a plane mirror.

In other words, the shortest distance between A and B via Q is the same as if A were on the other side of the wall at A′ and equidistant from O.

If **BD** is the perpendicular from B to AX.

Then the straight line A′QB gives the shortest distance, and by trigonometry:

$$\tan \text{BA'D} = \frac{\text{BD}}{\text{A'D}} = \frac{80 \sin 60°}{30+30+80 \cos 60°}$$

and the length OQ=30 tan BA′D=20.78 metres.

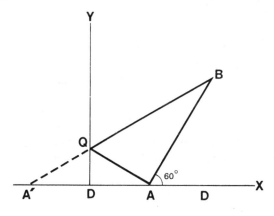

57 The census taker

The door number was 91. The reasoning is as follows:

1296 can be split into three factors in a variety of ways, and providing that each group of three factors always adds up to a different total then it would be a relatively simple matter for the census taker to have deduced the appropriate factors. She would have had no need for any further information, and this problem would have been solvable.

However, the fact that the man said that she would need the extra information about the number of cars implies that there was more than one way in which the door number could be expressed as the sum of three factors of 1296.

The only possible door number to conform to this criterion is 91, which can be made up in two ways:

1, 18, 72   and 2, 8, 81.

Hence the door number was 91.

58 A number crossword

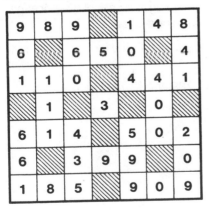

59 Another number crossword

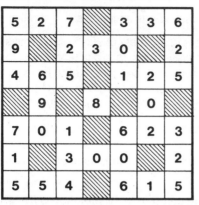

60 A sequence of primes

A straightforward slog, using the prime number generator subroutine that appears elsewhere in this text. However, you should want to restrict your searching as much as possible. For instance, if you want to see if there are two consecutive primes which add up to the required value, then clearly, their values are going to be about 53,000 each, so there'd be little point in starting the generation at 1.

Anyway, the answer is that the value of 106,620 can be made up of six consecutive prime numbers:

17,747 17,749 17,761 17,783 17,789 and 17,791.

61 The hymn board

J. J. Clessa's house number is 53 and his brother's door number is 27.

62 Three unusual digits

The three digits are 2, 4, and 8

63 A recurring quotient

1702—appears on 16 occasions

64 A rotating grid

4	8	2
1	5	7
6	3	9

65 The cocktail party

Annie was the Doctor,
Brian the Programmer,
Celia the Engineer,
Don the Accountant,
Erica the Teacher,
Frank the Solicitor.

A CATALOG OF SELECTED
DOVER BOOKS
IN ALL FIELDS OF INTEREST

A CATALOG OF SELECTED DOVER
BOOKS IN ALL FIELDS OF INTEREST

CONCERNING THE SPIRITUAL IN ART, Wassily Kandinsky. Pioneering work by father of abstract art. Thoughts on color theory, nature of art. Analysis of earlier masters. 12 illustrations. 80pp. of text. 5⅜ × 8½. 23411-8 Pa. $3.95

ANIMALS: 1,419 Copyright-Free Illustrations of Mammals, Birds, Fish, Insects, etc., Jim Harter (ed.). Clear wood engravings present, in extremely lifelike poses, over 1,000 species of animals. One of the most extensive pictorial sourcebooks of its kind. Captions. Index. 284pp. 9 × 12. 23766-4 Pa. $12.95

CELTIC ART: The Methods of Construction, George Bain. Simple geometric techniques for making Celtic interlacements, spirals, Kells-type initials, animals, humans, etc. Over 500 illustrations. 160pp. 9 × 12. (USO) 22923-8 Pa. $9.95

AN ATLAS OF ANATOMY FOR ARTISTS, Fritz Schider. Most thorough reference work on art anatomy in the world. Hundreds of illustrations, including selections from works by Vesalius, Leonardo, Goya, Ingres, Michelangelo, others. 593 illustrations. 192pp. 7⅛ × 10¼. 20241-0 Pa. $9.95

CELTIC HAND STROKE-BY-STROKE (Irish Half-Uncial from "The Book of Kells"): An Arthur Baker Calligraphy Manual, Arthur Baker. Complete guide to creating each letter of the alphabet in distinctive Celtic manner. Covers hand position, strokes, pens, inks, paper, more. Illustrated. 48pp. 8¼ × 11.
24336-2 Pa. $3.95

EASY ORIGAMI, John Montroll. Charming collection of 32 projects (hat, cup, pelican, piano, swan, many more) specially designed for the novice origami hobbyist. Clearly illustrated easy-to-follow instructions insure that even beginning papercrafters will achieve successful results. 48pp. 8¼ × 11. 27298-2 Pa. $2.95

THE COMPLETE BOOK OF BIRDHOUSE CONSTRUCTION FOR WOOD-WORKERS, Scott D. Campbell. Detailed instructions, illustrations, tables. Also data on bird habitat and instinct patterns. Bibliography. 3 tables. 63 illustrations in 15 figures. 48pp. 5¼ × 8½. 24407-5 Pa. $1.95

BLOOMINGDALE'S ILLUSTRATED 1886 CATALOG: Fashions, Dry Goods and Housewares, Bloomingdale Brothers. Famed merchants' extremely rare catalog depicting about 1,700 products: clothing, housewares, firearms, dry goods, jewelry, more. Invaluable for dating, identifying vintage items. Also, copyright-free graphics for artists, designers. Co-published with Henry Ford Museum & Green-field Village. 160pp. 8¼ × 11. 25780-0 Pa. $9.95

HISTORIC COSTUME IN PICTURES, Braun & Schneider. Over 1,450 costumed figures in clearly detailed engravings—from dawn of civilization to end of 19th century. Captions. Many folk costumes. 256pp. 8⅜ × 11¾. 23150-X Pa. $11.95

CATALOG OF DOVER BOOKS

STICKLEY CRAFTSMAN FURNITURE CATALOGS, Gustav Stickley and L. & J. G. Stickley. Beautiful, functional furniture in two authentic catalogs from 1910. 594 illustrations, including 277 photos, show settles, rockers, armchairs, reclining chairs, bookcases, desks, tables. 183pp. 6½ × 9¼. 23838-5 Pa. $9.95

AMERICAN LOCOMOTIVES IN HISTORIC PHOTOGRAPHS: 1858 to 1949, Ron Ziel (ed.). A rare collection of 126 meticulously detailed official photographs, called "builder portraits," of American locomotives that majestically chronicle the rise of steam locomotive power in America. Introduction. Detailed captions. xi + 129pp. 9 × 12. 27393-8 Pa. $12.95

AMERICA'S LIGHTHOUSES: An Illustrated History, Francis Ross Holland, Jr. Delightfully written, profusely illustrated fact-filled survey of over 200 American lighthouses since 1716. History, anecdotes, technological advances, more. 240pp. 8 × 10¾. 25576-X Pa. $11.95

TOWARDS A NEW ARCHITECTURE, Le Corbusier. Pioneering manifesto by founder of "International School." Technical and aesthetic theories, views of industry, economics, relation of form to function, "mass-production split" and much more. Profusely illustrated. 320pp. 6⅛ × 9¼. (USO) 25023-7 Pa. $9.95

HOW THE OTHER HALF LIVES, Jacob Riis. Famous journalistic record, exposing poverty and degradation of New York slums around 1900, by major social reformer. 100 striking and influential photographs. 233pp. 10 × 7⅞.
22012-5 Pa $10.95

FRUIT KEY AND TWIG KEY TO TREES AND SHRUBS, William M. Harlow. One of the handiest and most widely used identification aids. Fruit key covers 120 deciduous and evergreen species; twig key 160 deciduous species. Easily used. Over 300 photographs. 126pp. 5⅜ × 8½. 20511-8 Pa. $3.95

COMMON BIRD SONGS, Dr. Donald J. Borror. Songs of 60 most common U.S. birds: robins, sparrows, cardinals, bluejays, finches, more—arranged in order of increasing complexity. Up to 9 variations of songs of each species.
Cassette and manual 99911-4 $8.95

ORCHIDS AS HOUSE PLANTS, Rebecca Tyson Northen. Grow cattleyas and many other kinds of orchids—in a window, in a case, or under artificial light. 63 illustrations. 148pp. 5⅜ × 8½. 23261-1 Pa. $4.95

MONSTER MAZES, Dave Phillips. Masterful mazes at four levels of difficulty. Avoid deadly perils and evil creatures to find magical treasures. Solutions for all 32 exciting illustrated puzzles. 48pp. 8¼ × 11. 26005-4 Pa. $2.95

MOZART'S DON GIOVANNI (DOVER OPERA LIBRETTO SERIES), Wolfgang Amadeus Mozart. Introduced and translated by Ellen H. Bleiler. Standard Italian libretto, with complete English translation. Convenient and thoroughly portable—an ideal companion for reading along with a recording or the performance itself. Introduction. List of characters. Plot summary. 121pp. 5¼ × 8½.
24944-1 Pa. $2.95

TECHNICAL MANUAL AND DICTIONARY OF CLASSICAL BALLET, Gail Grant. Defines, explains, comments on steps, movements, poses and concepts. 15-page pictorial section. Basic book for student, viewer. 127pp. 5⅜ × 8½.
21843-0 Pa. $4.95

BRASS INSTRUMENTS: Their History and Development, Anthony Baines. Authoritative, updated survey of the evolution of trumpets, trombones, bugles, cornets, French horns, tubas and other brass wind instruments. Over 140 illustrations and 48 music examples. Corrected and updated by author. New preface. Bibliography. 320pp. 5⅜ × 8½. 27574-4 Pa. $9.95

HOLLYWOOD GLAMOR PORTRAITS, John Kobal (ed.). 145 photos from 1926–49. Harlow, Gable, Bogart, Bacall; 94 stars in all. Full background on photographers, technical aspects. 160pp. 8⅜ × 11¼. 23352-9 Pa. $11.95

MAX AND MORITZ, Wilhelm Busch. Great humor classic in both German and English. Also 10 other works: "Cat and Mouse," "Plisch and Plumm," etc. 216pp. 5⅜ × 8½. 20181-3 Pa. $5.95

THE RAVEN AND OTHER FAVORITE POEMS, Edgar Allan Poe. Over 40 of the author's most memorable poems: "The Bells," "Ulalume," "Israfel," "To Helen," "The Conqueror Worm," "Eldorado," "Annabel Lee," many more. Alphabetic lists of titles and first lines. 64pp. 5³⁄₁₆ × 8¼. 26685-0 Pa. $1.00

SEVEN SCIENCE FICTION NOVELS, H. G. Wells. The standard collection of the great novels. Complete, unabridged. First Men in the Moon, Island of Dr. Moreau, War of the Worlds, Food of the Gods, Invisible Man, Time Machine, In the Days of the Comet. Total of 1,015pp. 5⅜ × 8½. (USO) 20264-X Clothbd. $29.95

AMULETS AND SUPERSTITIONS, E. A. Wallis Budge. Comprehensive discourse on origin, powers of amulets in many ancient cultures: Arab, Persian, Babylonian, Assyrian, Egyptian, Gnostic, Hebrew, Phoenician, Syriac, etc. Covers cross, swastika, crucifix, seals, rings, stones, etc. 584pp. 5⅜ × 8½. 23573-4 Pa. $12.95

RUSSIAN STORIES/PYCCKNE PACCKA3bl: A Dual-Language Book, edited by Gleb Struve. Twelve tales by such masters as Chekhov, Tolstoy, Dostoevsky, Pushkin, others. Excellent word-for-word English translations on facing pages, plus teaching and study aids, Russian/English vocabulary, biographical/critical introductions, more. 416pp. 5⅜ × 8½. 26244-8 Pa. $8.95

PHILADELPHIA THEN AND NOW: 60 Sites Photographed in the Past and Present, Kenneth Finkel and Susan Oyama. Rare photographs of City Hall, Logan Square, Independence Hall, Betsy Ross House, other landmarks juxtaposed with contemporary views. Captures changing face of historic city. Introduction. Captions. 128pp. 8¼ × 11. 25790-8 Pa. $9.95

AIA ARCHITECTURAL GUIDE TO NASSAU AND SUFFOLK COUNTIES, LONG ISLAND, The American Institute of Architects, Long Island Chapter, and the Society for the Preservation of Long Island Antiquities. Comprehensive, well-researched and generously illustrated volume brings to life over three centuries of Long Island's great architectural heritage. More than 240 photographs with authoritative, extensively detailed captions. 176pp. 8¼ × 11. 26946-9 Pa. $14.95

NORTH AMERICAN INDIAN LIFE: Customs and Traditions of 23 Tribes, Elsie Clews Parsons (ed.). 27 fictionalized essays by noted anthropologists examine religion, customs, government, additional facets of life among the Winnebago, Crow, Zuni, Eskimo, other tribes. 480pp. 6⅛ × 9¼. 27377-6 Pa. $10.95

FRANK LLOYD WRIGHT'S HOLLYHOCK HOUSE, Donald Hoffmann. Lavishly illustrated, carefully documented study of one of Wright's most controversial residential designs. Over 120 photographs, floor plans, elevations, etc. Detailed perceptive text by noted Wright scholar. Index. 128pp. 9¼ × 10¾.
27133-1 Pa. $11.95

THE MALE AND FEMALE FIGURE IN MOTION: 60 Classic Photographic Sequences, Eadweard Muybridge. 60 true-action photographs of men and women walking, running, climbing, bending, turning, etc., reproduced from rare 19th-century masterpiece. vi + 121pp. 9 × 12. 24745-7 Pa. $10.95

1001 QUESTIONS ANSWERED ABOUT THE SEASHORE, N. J. Berrill and Jacquelyn Berrill. Queries answered about dolphins, sea snails, sponges, starfish, fishes, shore birds, many others. Covers appearance, breeding, growth, feeding, much more. 305pp. 5¼ × 8¼. 23366-9 Pa. $7.95

GUIDE TO OWL WATCHING IN NORTH AMERICA, Donald S. Heintzelman. Superb guide offers complete data and descriptions of 19 species: barn owl, screech owl, snowy owl, many more. Expert coverage of owl-watching equipment, conservation, migrations and invasions, etc. Guide to observing sites. 84 illustrations. xiii + 193pp. 5⅜ × 8½. 27344-X Pa. $8.95

MEDICINAL AND OTHER USES OF NORTH AMERICAN PLANTS: A Historical Survey with Special Reference to the Eastern Indian Tribes, Charlotte Erichsen-Brown. Chronological historical citations document 500 years of usage of plants, trees, shrubs native to eastern Canada, northeastern U.S. Also complete identifying information. 343 illustrations. 544pp. 6½ × 9¼. 25951-X Pa. $12.95

STORYBOOK MAZES, Dave Phillips. 23 stories and mazes on two-page spreads: Wizard of Oz, Treasure Island, Robin Hood, etc. Solutions. 64pp. 8¼ × 11.
23628-5 Pa. $2.95

NEGRO FOLK MUSIC, U.S.A., Harold Courlander. Noted folklorist's scholarly yet readable analysis of rich and varied musical tradition. Includes authentic versions of over 40 folk songs. Valuable bibliography and discography. xi + 324pp. 5⅜ × 8½. 27350-4 Pa. $7.95

MOVIE-STAR PORTRAITS OF THE FORTIES, John Kobal (ed.). 163 glamor, studio photos of 106 stars of the 1940s: Rita Hayworth, Ava Gardner, Marlon Brando, Clark Gable, many more. 176pp. 8⅜ × 11¼. 23546-7 Pa. $11.95

BENCHLEY LOST AND FOUND, Robert Benchley. Finest humor from early 30s, about pet peeves, child psychologists, post office and others. Mostly unavailable elsewhere. 73 illustrations by Peter Arno and others. 183pp. 5⅜ × 8½.
22410-4 Pa. $5.95

YEKL and THE IMPORTED BRIDEGROOM AND OTHER STORIES OF YIDDISH NEW YORK, Abraham Cahan. Film Hester Street based on Yekl (1896). Novel, other stories among first about Jewish immigrants on N.Y.'s East Side. 240pp. 5⅜ × 8½. 22427-9 Pa. $6.95

SELECTED POEMS, Walt Whitman. Generous sampling from *Leaves of Grass.* Twenty-four poems include "I Hear America Singing," "Song of the Open Road," "I Sing the Body Electric," "When Lilacs Last in the Dooryard Bloom'd," "O Captain! My Captain!"—all reprinted from an authoritative edition. Lists of titles and first lines. 128pp. 5³⁄₁₆ × 8¼. 26878-0 Pa. $1.00

THE BEST TALES OF HOFFMANN, E. T. A. Hoffmann. 10 of Hoffmann's most important stories: "Nutcracker and the King of Mice," "The Golden Flowerpot," etc. 458pp. 5⅜ × 8½. 21793-0 Pa. $8.95

FROM FETISH TO GOD IN ANCIENT EGYPT, E. A. Wallis Budge. Rich detailed survey of Egyptian conception of "God" and gods, magic, cult of animals, Osiris, more. Also, superb English translations of hymns and legends. 240 illustrations. 545pp. 5⅜ × 8½. 25803-3 Pa. $11.95

FRENCH STORIES/CONTES FRANÇAIS: A Dual-Language Book, Wallace Fowlie. Ten stories by French masters, Voltaire to Camus: "Micromegas" by Voltaire; "The Atheist's Mass" by Balzac; "Minuet" by de Maupassant; "The Guest" by Camus, six more. Excellent English translations on facing pages. Also French-English vocabulary list, exercises, more. 352pp. 5⅜ × 8½. 26443-2 Pa. $8.95

CHICAGO AT THE TURN OF THE CENTURY IN PHOTOGRAPHS: 122 Historic Views from the Collections of the Chicago Historical Society, Larry A. Viskochil. Rare large-format prints offer detailed views of City Hall, State Street, the Loop, Hull House, Union Station, many other landmarks, circa 1904–1913. Introduction. Captions. Maps. 144pp. 9⅜ × 12¼. 24656-6 Pa. $12.95

OLD BROOKLYN IN EARLY PHOTOGRAPHS, 1865–1929, William Lee Younger. Luna Park, Gravesend race track, construction of Grand Army Plaza, moving of Hotel Brighton, etc. 157 previously unpublished photographs. 165pp. 8⅞ × 11¾. 23587-4 Pa. $13.95

THE MYTHS OF THE NORTH AMERICAN INDIANS, Lewis Spence. Rich anthology of the myths and legends of the Algonquins, Iroquois, Pawnees and Sioux, prefaced by an extensive historical and ethnological commentary. 36 illustrations. 480pp. 5⅜ × 8½. 25967-6 Pa. $8.95

AN ENCYCLOPEDIA OF BATTLES: Accounts of Over 1,560 Battles from 1479 B.C. to the Present, David Eggenberger. Essential details of every major battle in recorded history from the first battle of Megiddo in 1479 B.C. to Grenada in 1984. List of Battle Maps. New Appendix covering the years 1967–1984. Index. 99 illustrations. 544pp. 6½ × 9¼. 24913-1 Pa. $14.95

SAILING ALONE AROUND THE WORLD, Captain Joshua Slocum. First man to sail around the world, alone, in small boat. One of great feats of seamanship told in delightful manner. 67 illustrations. 294pp. 5⅜ × 8½. 20326-3 Pa. $5.95

ANARCHISM AND OTHER ESSAYS, Emma Goldman. Powerful, penetrating, prophetic essays on direct action, role of minorities, prison reform, puritan hypocrisy, violence, etc. 271pp. 5⅜ × 8½. 22484-8 Pa. $5.95

MYTHS OF THE HINDUS AND BUDDHISTS, Ananda K. Coomaraswamy and Sister Nivedita. Great stories of the epics; deeds of Krishna, Shiva, taken from puranas, Vedas, folk tales; etc. 32 illustrations. 400pp. 5⅜ × 8½. 21759-0 Pa. $9.95

BEYOND PSYCHOLOGY, Otto Rank. Fear of death, desire of immortality, nature of sexuality, social organization, creativity, according to Rankian system. 291pp. 5⅜ × 8½. 20485-5 Pa. $8.95

A THEOLOGICO-POLITICAL TREATISE, Benedict Spinoza. Also contains unfinished Political Treatise. Great classic on religious liberty, theory of government on common consent. R. Elwes translation. Total of 421pp. 5⅜ × 8½. 20249-6 Pa. $8.95

MY BONDAGE AND MY FREEDOM, Frederick Douglass. Born a slave, Douglass became outspoken force in antislavery movement. The best of Douglass' autobiographies. Graphic description of slave life. 464pp. 5⅜ × 8½.   22457-0 Pa. $8.95

FOLLOWING THE EQUATOR: A Journey Around the World, Mark Twain. Fascinating humorous account of 1897 voyage to Hawaii, Australia, India, New Zealand, etc. Ironic, bemused reports on peoples, customs, climate, flora and fauna, politics, much more. 197 illustrations. 720pp. 5⅜ × 8½.   26113-1 Pa. $15.95

THE PEOPLE CALLED SHAKERS, Edward D. Andrews. Definitive study of Shakers: origins, beliefs, practices, dances, social organization, furniture and crafts, etc. 33 illustrations. 351pp. 5⅜ × 8½.   21081-2 Pa. $8.95

THE MYTHS OF GREECE AND ROME, H. A. Guerber. A classic of mythology, generously illustrated, long prized for its simple, graphic, accurate retelling of the principal myths of Greece and Rome, and for its commentary on their origins and significance. With 64 illustrations by Michelangelo, Raphael, Titian, Rubens, Canova, Bernini and others. 480pp. 5⅜ × 8½.   27584-1 Pa. $9.95

PSYCHOLOGY OF MUSIC, Carl E. Seashore. Classic work discusses music as a medium from psychological viewpoint. Clear treatment of physical acoustics, auditory apparatus, sound perception, development of musical skills, nature of musical feeling, host of other topics. 88 figures. 408pp. 5⅜ × 8½. 21851-1 Pa. $9.95

THE PHILOSOPHY OF HISTORY, Georg W. Hegel. Great classic of Western thought develops concept that history is not chance but rational process, the evolution of freedom. 457pp. 5⅜ × 8½.   20112-0 Pa. $9.95

THE BOOK OF TEA, Kakuzo Okakura. Minor classic of the Orient: entertaining, charming explanation, interpretation of traditional Japanese culture in terms of tea ceremony. 94pp. 5⅜ × 8½.   20070-1 Pa. $3.95

LIFE IN ANCIENT EGYPT, Adolf Erman. Fullest, most thorough, detailed older account with much not in more recent books, domestic life, religion, magic, medicine, commerce, much more. Many illustrations reproduce tomb paintings, carvings, hieroglyphs, etc. 597pp. 5⅜ × 8½.   22632-8 Pa. $10.95

SUNDIALS, Their Theory and Construction, Albert Waugh. Far and away the best, most thorough coverage of ideas, mathematics concerned, types, construction, adjusting anywhere. Simple, nontechnical treatment allows even children to build several of these dials. Over 100 illustrations. 230pp. 5⅜ × 8½.   22947-5 Pa. $7.95

DYNAMICS OF FLUIDS IN POROUS MEDIA, Jacob Bear. For advanced students of ground water hydrology, soil mechanics and physics, drainage and irrigation engineering, and more. 335 illustrations. Exercises, with answers. 784pp. 6⅛ × 9¼.   65675-6 Pa. $19.95

SONGS OF EXPERIENCE: Facsimile Reproduction with 26 Plates in Full Color, William Blake. 26 full-color plates from a rare 1826 edition. Includes "The Tyger," "London," "Holy Thursday," and other poems. Printed text of poems. 48pp. 5¼ × 7.   24636-1 Pa. $4.95

OLD-TIME VIGNETTES IN FULL COLOR, Carol Belanger Grafton (ed.). Over 390 charming, often sentimental illustrations, selected from archives of Victorian graphics—pretty women posing, children playing, food, flowers, kittens and puppies, smiling cherubs, birds and butterflies, much more. All copyright-free. 48pp. 9¼ × 12¼.   27269-9 Pa. $5.95

PERSPECTIVE FOR ARTISTS, Rex Vicat Cole. Depth, perspective of sky and sea, shadows, much more, not usually covered. 391 diagrams, 81 reproductions of drawings and paintings. 279pp. 5⅜ × 8½. 22487-2 Pa. $6.95

DRAWING THE LIVING FIGURE, Joseph Sheppard. Innovative approach to artistic anatomy focuses on specifics of surface anatomy, rather than muscles and bones. Over 170 drawings of live models in front, back and side views, and in widely varying poses. Accompanying diagrams. 177 illustrations. Introduction. Index. 144pp. 8⅜ × 11¼. 26723-7 Pa. $8.95

GOTHIC AND OLD ENGLISH ALPHABETS: 100 Complete Fonts, Dan X. Solo. Add power, elegance to posters, signs, other graphics with 100 stunning copyright-free alphabets: Blackstone, Dolbey, Germania, 97 more—including many lower-case, numerals, punctuation marks. 104pp. 8⅛ × 11. 24695-7 Pa. $8.95

HOW TO DO BEADWORK, Mary White. Fundamental book on craft from simple projects to five-bead chains and woven works. 106 illustrations. 142pp. 5⅜ × 8. 20697-1 Pa. $4.95

THE BOOK OF WOOD CARVING, Charles Marshall Sayers. Finest book for beginners discusses fundamentals and offers 34 designs. "Absolutely first rate . . . well thought out and well executed."—E. J. Tangerman. 118pp. 7¾ × 10⅝. 23654-4 Pa. $5.95

ILLUSTRATED CATALOG OF CIVIL WAR MILITARY GOODS: Union Army Weapons, Insignia, Uniform Accessories, and Other Equipment, Schuyler, Hartley, and Graham. Rare, profusely illustrated 1846 catalog includes Union Army uniform and dress regulations, arms and ammunition, coats, insignia, flags, swords, rifles, etc. 226 illustrations. 160pp. 9 × 12. 24939-5 Pa. $10.95

WOMEN'S FASHIONS OF THE EARLY 1900s: An Unabridged Republication of "New York Fashions, 1909," National Cloak & Suit Co. Rare catalog of mail-order fashions documents women's and children's clothing styles shortly after the turn of the century. Captions offer full descriptions, prices. Invaluable resource for fashion, costume historians. Approximately 725 illustrations. 128pp. 8⅜ × 11¼. 27276-1 Pa. $11.95

THE 1912 AND 1915 GUSTAV STICKLEY FURNITURE CATALOGS, Gustav Stickley. With over 200 detailed illustrations and descriptions, these two catalogs are essential reading and reference materials and identification guides for Stickley furniture. Captions cite materials, dimensions and prices. 112pp. 6½ × 9¼. 26676-1 Pa. $9.95

EARLY AMERICAN LOCOMOTIVES, John H. White, Jr. Finest locomotive engravings from early 19th century: historical (1804–74), main-line (after 1870), special, foreign, etc. 147 plates. 142pp. 11⅜ × 8¼. 22772-3 Pa. $10.95

THE TALL SHIPS OF TODAY IN PHOTOGRAPHS, Frank O. Braynard. Lavishly illustrated tribute to nearly 100 majestic contemporary sailing vessels: Amerigo Vespucci, Clearwater, Constitution, Eagle, Mayflower, Sea Cloud, Victory, many more. Authoritative captions provide statistics, background on each ship. 190 black-and-white photographs and illustrations. Introduction. 128pp. 8⅞ × 11¾. 27163-3 Pa. $13.95

EARLY NINETEENTH-CENTURY CRAFTS AND TRADES, Peter Stockham (ed.). Extremely rare 1807 volume describes to youngsters the crafts and trades of the day: brickmaker, weaver, dressmaker, bookbinder, ropemaker, saddler, many more. Quaint prose, charming illustrations for each craft. 20 black-and-white line illustrations. 192pp. 4⅜ × 6. 27293-1 Pa. $4.95

VICTORIAN FASHIONS AND COSTUMES FROM HARPER'S BAZAR, 1867-1898, Stella Blum (ed.). Day costumes, evening wear, sports clothes, shoes, hats, other accessories in over 1,000 detailed engravings. 320pp. 9⅜ × 12¼. 22990-4 Pa. $13.95

GUSTAV STICKLEY, THE CRAFTSMAN, Mary Ann Smith. Superb study surveys broad scope of Stickley's achievement, especially in architecture. Design philosophy, rise and fall of the Craftsman empire, descriptions and floor plans for many Craftsman houses, more. 86 black-and-white halftones. 31 line illustrations. Introduction. 208pp. 6½ × 9¼. 27210-9 Pa. $9.95

THE LONG ISLAND RAIL ROAD IN EARLY PHOTOGRAPHS, Ron Ziel. Over 220 rare photos, informative text document origin (1844) and development of rail service on Long Island. Vintage views of early trains, locomotives, stations, passengers, crews, much more. Captions. 8⅞ × 11¾. 26301-0 Pa. $13.95

THE BOOK OF OLD SHIPS: From Egyptian Galleys to Clipper Ships, Henry B. Culver. Superb, authoritative history of sailing vessels, with 80 magnificent line illustrations. Galley, bark, caravel, longship, whaler, many more. Detailed, informative text on each vessel by noted naval historian. Introduction. 256pp. 5⅜ × 8½. 27332-6 Pa. $6.95

TEN BOOKS ON ARCHITECTURE, Vitruvius. The most important book ever written on architecture. Early Roman aesthetics, technology, classical orders, site selection, all other aspects. Morgan translation. 331pp. 5⅜ × 8½. 20645-9 Pa. $8.95

THE HUMAN FIGURE IN MOTION, Eadweard Muybridge. More than 4,500 stopped-action photos, in action series, showing undraped men, women, children jumping, lying down, throwing, sitting, wrestling, carrying, etc. 390pp. 7⅞ × 10⅝. 20204-6 Clothbd. $24.95

TREES OF THE EASTERN AND CENTRAL UNITED STATES AND CANADA, William M. Harlow. Best one-volume guide to 140 trees. Full descriptions, woodlore, range, etc. Over 600 illustrations. Handy size. 288pp. 4½ × 6⅜. 20395-6 Pa. $5.95

SONGS OF WESTERN BIRDS, Dr. Donald J. Borror. Complete song and call repertoire of 60 western species, including flycatchers, juncoes, cactus wrens, many more—includes fully illustrated booklet. Cassette and manual 99913-0 $8.95

GROWING AND USING HERBS AND SPICES, Milo Miloradovich. Versatile handbook provides all the information needed for cultivation and use of all the herbs and spices available in North America. 4 illustrations. Index. Glossary. 236pp. 5⅜ × 8½. 25058-X Pa. $6.95

BIG BOOK OF MAZES AND LABYRINTHS, Walter Shepherd. 50 mazes and labyrinths in all—classical, solid, ripple, and more—in one great volume. Perfect inexpensive puzzler for clever youngsters. Full solutions. 112pp. 8⅛ × 11. 22951-3 Pa. $4.95

CATALOG OF DOVER BOOKS

PIANO TUNING, J. Cree Fischer. Clearest, best book for beginner, amateur. Simple repairs, raising dropped notes, tuning by easy method of flattened fifths. No previous skills needed. 4 illustrations. 201pp. 5⅜ × 8½.   23267-0 Pa. $5.95

A SOURCE BOOK IN THEATRICAL HISTORY, A. M. Nagler. Contemporary observers on acting, directing, make-up, costuming, stage props, machinery, scene design, from Ancient Greece to Chekhov. 611pp. 5⅜ × 8½.   20515-0 Pa. $11.95

THE COMPLETE NONSENSE OF EDWARD LEAR, Edward Lear. All nonsense limericks, zany alphabets, Owl and Pussycat, songs, nonsense botany, etc., illustrated by Lear. Total of 320pp. 5⅜ × 8½. (USO)   20167-8 Pa. $6.95

VICTORIAN PARLOUR POETRY: An Annotated Anthology, Michael R. Turner. 117 gems by Longfellow, Tennyson, Browning, many lesser-known poets. "The Village Blacksmith," "Curfew Must Not Ring Tonight," "Only a Baby Small," dozens more, often difficult to find elsewhere. Index of poets, titles, first lines. xxiii + 325pp. 5⅜ × 8¼.   27044-0 Pa. $8.95

DUBLINERS, James Joyce. Fifteen stories offer vivid, tightly focused observations of the lives of Dublin's poorer classes. At least one, "The Dead," is considered a masterpiece. Reprinted complete and unabridged from standard edition. 160pp. 5³⁄₁₆ × 8¼.   26870-5 Pa. $1.00

THE HAUNTED MONASTERY and THE CHINESE MAZE MURDERS, Robert van Gulik. Two full novels by van Gulik, set in 7th-century China, continue adventures of Judge Dee and his companions. An evil Taoist monastery, seemingly supernatural events; overgrown topiary maze hides strange crimes. 27 illustrations. 328pp. 5⅜ × 8½.   23502-5 Pa. $7.95

THE BOOK OF THE SACRED MAGIC OF ABRAMELIN THE MAGE, translated by S. MacGregor Mathers. Medieval manuscript of ceremonial magic. Basic document in Aleister Crowley, Golden Dawn groups. 268pp. 5⅜ × 8½.   23211-5 Pa. $8.95

NEW RUSSIAN-ENGLISH AND ENGLISH-RUSSIAN DICTIONARY, M. A. O'Brien. This is a remarkably handy Russian dictionary, containing a surprising amount of information, including over 70,000 entries. 366pp. 4½ × 6⅛.   20208-9 Pa. $9.95

HISTORIC HOMES OF THE AMERICAN PRESIDENTS, Second, Revised Edition, Irvin Haas. A traveler's guide to American Presidential homes, most open to the public, depicting and describing homes occupied by every American President from George Washington to George Bush. With visiting hours, admission charges, travel routes. 175 photographs. Index. 160pp. 8¼ × 11. 26751-2 Pa. $10.95

NEW YORK IN THE FORTIES, Andreas Feininger. 162 brilliant photographs by the well-known photographer, formerly with *Life* magazine. Commuters, shoppers, Times Square at night, much else from city at its peak. Captions by John von Hartz. 181pp. 9¼ × 10¾.   23585-8 Pa. $12.95

INDIAN SIGN LANGUAGE, William Tomkins. Over 525 signs developed by Sioux and other tribes. Written instructions and diagrams. Also 290 pictographs. 111pp. 6⅛ × 9¼.   22029-X Pa. $3.50

ANATOMY: A Complete Guide for Artists, Joseph Sheppard. A master of figure drawing shows artists how to render human anatomy convincingly. Over 460 illustrations. 224pp. 8⅜ × 11¼. 27279-6 Pa. $10.95

MEDIEVAL CALLIGRAPHY: Its History and Technique, Marc Drogin. Spirited history, comprehensive instruction manual covers 13 styles (ca. 4th century thru 15th). Excellent photographs; directions for duplicating medieval techniques with modern tools. 224pp. 8⅜ × 11¼. 26142-5 Pa. $11.95

DRIED FLOWERS: How to Prepare Them, Sarah Whitlock and Martha Rankin. Complete instructions on how to use silica gel, meal and borax, perlite aggregate, sand and borax, glycerine and water to create attractive permanent flower arrangements. 12 illustrations. 32pp. 5⅜ × 8½. 21802-3 Pa. $1.00

EASY-TO-MAKE BIRD FEEDERS FOR WOODWORKERS, Scott D. Campbell. Detailed, simple-to-use guide for designing, constructing, caring for and using feeders. Text, illustrations for 12 classic and contemporary designs. 96pp. 5⅜ × 8½. 25847-5 Pa. $2.95

OLD-TIME CRAFTS AND TRADES, Peter Stockham. An 1807 book created to teach children about crafts and trades open to them as future careers. It describes in detailed, nontechnical terms 24 different occupations, among them coachmaker, gardener, hairdresser, lacemaker, shoemaker, wheelwright, copper-plate printer, milliner, trunkmaker, merchant and brewer. Finely detailed engravings illustrate each occupation. 192pp. 4⅝ × 6. 27398-9 Pa. $4.95

THE HISTORY OF UNDERCLOTHES, C. Willett Cunnington and Phyllis Cunnington. Fascinating, well-documented survey covering six centuries of English undergarments, enhanced with over 100 illustrations: 12th-century laced-up bodice, footed long drawers (1795), 19th-century bustles, 19th-century corsets for men, Victorian "bust improvers," much more. 272pp. 5⅜ × 8¼. 27124-2 Pa. $9.95

ARTS AND CRAFTS FURNITURE: The Complete Brooks Catalog of 1912, Brooks Manufacturing Co. Photos and detailed descriptions of more than 150 now very collectible furniture designs from the Arts and Crafts movement depict davenports, settees, buffets, desks, tables, chairs, bedsteads, dressers and more, all built of solid, quarter-sawed oak. Invaluable for students and enthusiasts of antiques, Americana and the decorative arts. 80pp. 6½ × 9¼. 27471-3 Pa. $7.95

HOW WE INVENTED THE AIRPLANE: An Illustrated History, Orville Wright. Fascinating firsthand account covers early experiments, construction of planes and motors, first flights, much more. Introduction and commentary by Fred C. Kelly. 76 photographs. 96pp. 8¼ × 11. 25662-6 Pa. $8.95

THE ARTS OF THE SAILOR: Knotting, Splicing and Ropework, Hervey Garrett Smith. Indispensable shipboard reference covers tools, basic knots and useful hitches; handsewing and canvas work, more. Over 100 illustrations. Delightful reading for sea lovers. 256pp. 5⅜ × 8½. 26440-8 Pa. $7.95

FRANK LLOYD WRIGHT'S FALLINGWATER: The House and Its History, Second, Revised Edition, Donald Hoffmann. A total revision—both in text and illustrations—of the standard document on Fallingwater, the boldest, most personal architectural statement of Wright's mature years, updated with valuable new material from the recently opened Frank Lloyd Wright Archives. "Fascinating"—*The New York Times.* 116 illustrations. 128pp. 9¼ × 10¾. 27430-6 Pa. $10.95

CATALOG OF DOVER BOOKS

PHOTOGRAPHIC SKETCHBOOK OF THE CIVIL WAR, Alexander Gardner. 100 photos taken on field during the Civil War. Famous shots of Manassas, Harper's Ferry, Lincoln, Richmond, slave pens, etc. 244pp. 10⅝ × 8¼.
22731-6 Pa. $9.95

FIVE ACRES AND INDEPENDENCE, Maurice G. Kains. Great back-to-the-land classic explains basics of self-sufficient farming. The one book to get. 95 illustrations. 397pp. 5⅜ × 8½.
20974-1 Pa. $7.95

SONGS OF EASTERN BIRDS, Dr. Donald J. Borror. Songs and calls of 60 species most common to eastern U.S.: warblers, woodpeckers, flycatchers, thrushes, larks, many more in high-quality recording.
Cassette and manual 99912-2 $8.95

A MODERN HERBAL, Margaret Grieve. Much the fullest, most exact, most useful compilation of herbal material. Gigantic alphabetical encyclopedia, from aconite to zedoary, gives botanical information, medical properties, folklore, economic uses, much else. Indispensable to serious reader. 161 illustrations. 888pp. 6½ × 9¼.
2-vol. set. (USO)
Vol. I: 22798-7 Pa. $9.95
Vol. II: 22799-5 Pa. $9.95

HIDDEN TREASURE MAZE BOOK, Dave Phillips. Solve 34 challenging mazes accompanied by heroic tales of adventure. Evil dragons, people-eating plants, bloodthirsty giants, many more dangerous adversaries lurk at every twist and turn. 34 mazes, stories, solutions. 48pp. 8¼ × 11.
24566-7 Pa. $2.95

LETTERS OF W. A. MOZART, Wolfgang A. Mozart. Remarkable letters show bawdy wit, humor, imagination, musical insights, contemporary musical world; includes some letters from Leopold Mozart. 276pp. 5⅜ × 8½.
22859-2 Pa. $7.95

BASIC PRINCIPLES OF CLASSICAL BALLET, Agrippina Vaganova. Great Russian theoretician, teacher explains methods for teaching classical ballet. 118 illustrations. 175pp. 5⅜ × 8½.
22036-2 Pa. $4.95

THE JUMPING FROG, Mark Twain. Revenge edition. The original story of The Celebrated Jumping Frog of Calaveras County, a hapless French translation, and Twain's hilarious "retranslation" from the French. 12 illustrations. 66pp. 5⅜ × 8½.
22686-7 Pa. $3.95

BEST REMEMBERED POEMS, Martin Gardner (ed.). The 126 poems in this superb collection of 19th- and 20th-century British and American verse range from Shelley's "To a Skylark" to the impassioned "Renascence" of Edna St. Vincent Millay and to Edward Lear's whimsical "The Owl and the Pussycat." 224pp. 5⅜ × 8½.
27165-X Pa. $4.95

COMPLETE SONNETS, William Shakespeare. Over 150 exquisite poems deal with love, friendship, the tyranny of time, beauty's evanescence, death and other themes in language of remarkable power, precision and beauty. Glossary of archaic terms. 80pp. 5³⁄₁₆ × 8¼.
26686-9 Pa. $1.00

BODIES IN A BOOKSHOP, R. T. Campbell. Challenging mystery of blackmail and murder with ingenious plot and superbly drawn characters. In the best tradition of British suspense fiction. 192pp. 5⅜ × 8½.
24720-1 Pa. $5.95

THE WIT AND HUMOR OF OSCAR WILDE, Alvin Redman (ed.). More than 1,000 ripostes, paradoxes, wisecracks: Work is the curse of the drinking classes; I can resist everything except temptation; etc. 258pp. 5⅜ × 8½. 20602-5 Pa. $5.95

SHAKESPEARE LEXICON AND QUOTATION DICTIONARY, Alexander Schmidt. Full definitions, locations, shades of meaning in every word in plays and poems. More than 50,000 exact quotations. 1,485pp. 6½ × 9¼. 2-vol. set.
Vol. I: 22726-X Pa. $16.95
Vol. 2: 22727-8 Pa. $15.95

SELECTED POEMS, Emily Dickinson. Over 100 best-known, best-loved poems by one of America's foremost poets, reprinted from authoritative early editions. No comparable edition at this price. Index of first lines. 64pp. 5³⁄₁₆ × 8¼.
26466-1 Pa. $1.00

CELEBRATED CASES OF JUDGE DEE (DEE GOONG AN), translated by Robert van Gulik. Authentic 18th-century Chinese detective novel; Dee and associates solve three interlocked cases. Led to van Gulik's own stories with same characters. Extensive introduction. 9 illustrations. 237pp. 5⅜ × 8½.
23337-5 Pa. $6.95

THE MALLEUS MALEFICARUM OF KRAMER AND SPRENGER, translated by Montague Summers. Full text of most important witchhunter's "bible," used by both Catholics and Protestants. 278pp. 6⅝ × 10. 22802-9 Pa. $11.95

SPANISH STORIES/CUENTOS ESPAÑOLES: A Dual-Language Book, Angel Flores (ed.). Unique format offers 13 great stories in Spanish by Cervantes, Borges, others. Faithful English translations on facing pages. 352pp. 5⅜ × 8½.
25399-6 Pa. $8.95

THE CHICAGO WORLD'S FAIR OF 1893: A Photographic Record, Stanley Appelbaum (ed.). 128 rare photos show 200 buildings, Beaux-Arts architecture, Midway, original Ferris Wheel, Edison's kinetoscope, more. Architectural emphasis; full text. 116pp. 8¼ × 11. 23990-X Pa. $9.95

OLD QUEENS, N.Y., IN EARLY PHOTOGRAPHS, Vincent F. Seyfried and William Asadorian. Over 160 rare photographs of Maspeth, Jamaica, Jackson Heights, and other areas. Vintage views of DeWitt Clinton mansion, 1939 World's Fair and more. Captions. 192pp. 8⅞ × 11. 26358-4 Pa. $12.95

CAPTURED BY THE INDIANS: 15 Firsthand Accounts, 1750-1870, Frederick Drimmer. Astounding true historical accounts of grisly torture, bloody conflicts, relentless pursuits, miraculous escapes and more, by people who lived to tell the tale. 384pp. 5⅜ × 8½. 24901-8 Pa. $8.95

THE WORLD'S GREAT SPEECHES, Lewis Copeland and Lawrence W. Lamm (eds.). Vast collection of 278 speeches of Greeks to 1970. Powerful and effective models; unique look at history. 842pp. 5⅜ × 8½. 20468-5 Pa. $14.95

THE BOOK OF THE SWORD, Sir Richard F. Burton. Great Victorian scholar/adventurer's eloquent, erudite history of the "queen of weapons"—from prehistory to early Roman Empire. Evolution and development of early swords, variations (sabre, broadsword, cutlass, scimitar, etc.), much more. 336pp. 6⅛ × 9¼. 25434-8 Pa. $8.95

AUTOBIOGRAPHY: The Story of My Experiments with Truth, Mohandas K. Gandhi. Boyhood, legal studies, purification, the growth of the Satyagraha (nonviolent protest) movement. Critical, inspiring work of the man responsible for the freedom of India. 480pp. 5⅜ × 8½. (USO) 24593-4 Pa. $8.95

CELTIC MYTHS AND LEGENDS, T. W. Rolleston. Masterful retelling of Irish and Welsh stories and tales. Cuchulain, King Arthur, Deirdre, the Grail, many more. First paperback edition. 58 full-page illustrations. 512pp. 5⅜ × 8½.
26507-2 Pa. $9.95

THE PRINCIPLES OF PSYCHOLOGY, William James. Famous long course complete, unabridged. Stream of thought, time perception, memory, experimental methods; great work decades ahead of its time. 94 figures. 1,391pp. 5⅜ × 8½. 2-vol. set.
Vol. I: 20381-6 Pa. $12.95
Vol. II: 20382-4 Pa. $12.95

THE WORLD AS WILL AND REPRESENTATION, Arthur Schopenhauer. Definitive English translation of Schopenhauer's life work, correcting more than 1,000 errors, omissions in earlier translations. Translated by E. F. J. Payne. Total of 1,269pp. 5⅜ × 8½. 2-vol. set. Vol. 1: 21761-2 Pa. $11.95
Vol. 2: 21762-0 Pa. $11.95

MAGIC AND MYSTERY IN TIBET, Madame Alexandra David-Neel. Experiences among lamas, magicians, sages, sorcerers, Bonpa wizards. A true psychic discovery. 32 illustrations. 321pp. 5⅜ × 8½. (USO) 22682-4 Pa. $8.95

THE EGYPTIAN BOOK OF THE DEAD, E. A. Wallis Budge. Complete reproduction of Ani's papyrus, finest ever found. Full hieroglyphic text, interlinear transliteration, word-for-word translation, smooth translation. 533pp. 6½ × 9¼.
21866-X Pa. $9.95

MATHEMATICS FOR THE NONMATHEMATICIAN, Morris Kline. Detailed, college-level treatment of mathematics in cultural and historical context, with numerous exercises. Recommended Reading Lists. Tables. Numerous figures. 641pp. 5⅜ × 8½. 24823-2 Pa. $11.95

THEORY OF WING SECTIONS: Including a Summary of Airfoil Data, Ira H. Abbott and A. E. von Doenhoff. Concise compilation of subsonic aerodynamic characteristics of NACA wing sections, plus description of theory. 350pp. of tables. 693pp. 5⅜ × 8½. 60586-8 Pa. $14.95

THE RIME OF THE ANCIENT MARINER, Gustave Doré, S. T. Coleridge. Doré's finest work; 34 plates capture moods, subtleties of poem. Flawless full-size reproductions printed on facing pages with authoritative text of poem. "Beautiful. Simply beautiful."—*Publisher's Weekly*. 77pp. 9¼ × 12. 22305-1 Pa. $6.95

NORTH AMERICAN INDIAN DESIGNS FOR ARTISTS AND CRAFTS-PEOPLE, Eva Wilson. Over 360 authentic copyright-free designs adapted from Navajo blankets, Hopi pottery, Sioux buffalo hides, more. Geometrics, symbolic figures, plant and animal motifs, etc. 128pp. 8⅜ × 11. (EUK) 25341-4 Pa. $7.95

SCULPTURE: Principles and Practice, Louis Slobodkin. Step-by-step approach to clay, plaster, metals, stone; classical and modern. 253 drawings, photos. 255pp. 8⅛ × 11. 22960-2 Pa. $10.95

THE INFLUENCE OF SEA POWER UPON HISTORY, 1660–1783, A. T. Mahan. Influential classic of naval history and tactics still used as text in war colleges. First paperback edition. 4 maps. 24 battle plans. 640pp. 5⅜ × 8½. 25509-3 Pa. $12.95

THE STORY OF THE TITANIC AS TOLD BY ITS SURVIVORS, Jack Winocour (ed.). What it was really like. Panic, despair, shocking inefficiency, and a little heroism. More thrilling than any fictional account. 26 illustrations. 320pp. 5⅜ × 8½. 20610-6 Pa. $8.95

FAIRY AND FOLK TALES OF THE IRISH PEASANTRY, William Butler Yeats (ed.). Treasury of 64 tales from the twilight world of Celtic myth and legend: "The Soul Cages," "The Kildare Pooka," "King O'Toole and his Goose," many more. Introduction and Notes by W. B. Yeats. 352pp. 5⅜ × 8½. 26941-8 Pa. $8.95

BUDDHIST MAHAYANA TEXTS, E. B. Cowell and Others (eds.). Superb, accurate translations of basic documents in Mahayana Buddhism, highly important in history of religions. The Buddha-karita of Asvaghosha, Larger Sukhavativyuha, more. 448pp. 5⅜ × 8½. 25552-2 Pa. $9.95

ONE TWO THREE . . . INFINITY: Facts and Speculations of Science, George Gamow. Great physicist's fascinating, readable overview of contemporary science: number theory, relativity, fourth dimension, entropy, genes, atomic structure, much more. 128 illustrations. Index. 352pp. 5⅜ × 8½. 25664-2 Pa. $8.95

ENGINEERING IN HISTORY, Richard Shelton Kirby, et al. Broad, nontechnical survey of history's major technological advances: birth of Greek science, industrial revolution, electricity and applied science, 20th-century automation, much more. 181 illustrations. ". . . excellent . . ."—*Isis*. Bibliography. vii + 530pp. 5⅜ × 8¼. 26412-2 Pa. $14.95

Prices subject to change without notice.

Available at your book dealer or write for free catalog to Dept. GI, Dover Publications, Inc., 31 East 2nd St., Mineola, N.Y. 11501. Dover publishes more than 500 books each year on science, elementary and advanced mathematics, biology, music, art, literary history, social sciences and other areas.